My Father: A Remembrance

My Father:
A Remembrance

Hugo Black, Jr.

Random House
New York

All rights reserved under International and Pan-American Copyright Conven-
tions. Published in the United States by Random House, Inc., New York, and
simultaneously in Canada by Random House of Canada Limited, Toronto.

Grateful acknowledgment is made to Chappell & Co., Inc for permission to
reprint one line of lyrics from "A Hymn to Him" (page 123). Copyright © 1956
by Alan Jay Lerner and Frederick Loewe. All rights reserved.

Library of Congress Cataloging in Publication Data

Black, Hugo, 1922–
  My father, a remembrance.

  1. Black, Hugo Lafayette, 1886–1971. I. Title.
KF8745.B55B55   347'.73'2634 [B]   75 12410
ISBN 0–394–49631–0

Manufactured in the United States of America
98765432
First Edition

*To Graham and Mama
and my father, Hugo Black*

Preface

This book is not intended to be a chronicle of the major events in the life of Justice Hugo L. Black or a study of his social and political achievements and failures. I have done very little research; almost everything has been dredged from my own memory and filtered through my perception. After I am through, much will be left to be said about my father's life by historians and by those, like me, who have treasured their relationship with him. In short, what I am trying to do is to simply tell the story of a father and son moving toward each other.

If my father were alive now and knew about this book, I suppose he would not react very favorably. He was always afraid that if historians knew too much about the personal life of a justice, their interpretation of history might be distorted. Moreover, he always tried to avoid testimonials of any kind and took a dim view of any sort of flattery or public accolade. Even toward the end of his life he refused to allow anyone to paint his portrait or sculpt a bust of him. "Son," he would say, "this business of paintings and busts and that kind of stuff is bad business. Fella that yields to it is getting in dangerous territory. He's beginning to believe these nuts telling him he's some kind of godlike fella."

In a way, I guess you might say I am writing this book in spite of my father's desire that he be remembered only through his official acts—the laws he introduced and the opinions he wrote. But I feel that my story of a unique father-son relationship is important in its own way and should be told. It was not always easy being the son of a famous man, and many times I was hurt by his harsh criticism. Nevertheless, by learning to love and understand him, I was left with a genuine sense of my own worth.

My Father: A Remembrance

Boyhood in Clay County

Daddy was born at the family home in a remote area of Alabama—a little place called Harlan, which was about ten miles out from the Clay County seat of Ashland. Clay County itself is situated in the eastern part of the state, off the beaten path. As my father used to say, "Paris" to a Clay County boy was Taladega, the county seat of Taladega County. In those days there was rarely any doctor within treating distance of anybody in the county, and, aptly enough, the Baptist church in Ashland was called the Primitive Baptist Church.

Hugo was the baby of his family, the eighth and last child of William Lafayette Black and Martha Ardella Tolland Black. He was born on February 27, 1886, about a week after his three-year-old sister Della died. His mother apparently felt special tenderness for him because his birth had relieved her grief over the death of little Della, whom she had "laid to rest on Mount A-rat" (the Clay County pronunciation of Ararat).

I never knew either of my father's parents. By the time

I came along, my grandmother and grandfather had been dead for nearly twenty-five years. Pictures of my father's father, taken just a couple of years before his death when he was fifty, show an extraordinarily handsome man. Yet, from what Daddy told me, his mother married on the rebound. She had been in love with my grandfather's brother, Columbus, who had fought gallantly with Lee all the way to Gettysburg. There he participated in Pickett's Charge, flinging himself recklessly up the hill, until suddenly, near the top, the Yankees cut him down. When he got the slug, he threw up his hands, flung his gun away, exclaimed, "Oh Lordy, Oh Lordy," and dropped in his tracks, never to rise again.

Columbus was apparently the first love of Della Black, the love of her life. I don't think Della ever really respected my grandfather, much less loved him. He had a terrible drinking problem, which didn't contribute anything to an already shaky marriage. Her attitude toward her husband no doubt affected Daddy, who soon began to regard his father as nothing but a well-functioning spree drinker. His father would go on drinking sprees for days at a time, his wife all the while trying to dry him out so he could get back to the store he was running. The only time he was ever sober, Daddy thought, was when the liquor had run out.

Although Daddy respected his father as a businessman, it seems he could not respect him as a human being. I really believe that somewhere along the line my father even went so far as to change his name so he wouldn't be called the same thing as his father. I learned after his death that the family Bible carried his name as "Lafayette

Hugo Black," which later he seems to have changed to Hugo Lafayette. His father was called Fayette—pronounced "Fate," in Clay County.

Daddy's attitude toward his father was not a matter of hate or active dislike—simply one of cold indifference. Whatever it was, Fate never got through to his youngest child, who remembered his mother, Della, with worship and always felt that he was Della's favorite. He said he never walked out of the house without her inspecting him —straightening him up and sending him out "the neatest boy in Clay County."

It was plain to everyone that even though Hugo didn't look up to his father, he did as a boy greatly admire his four older brothers, Lee, Orlando, Pelham and Vernon. When Vernon, whom he idolized, died of typhoid fever at the age of seventeen, he turned to Pelham, who became to him a very special person. He was smart, and with his slender muscular build, he excelled in sports. He reportedly studied for the Alabama bar exam in the woods and received the highest grade anybody had ever gotten up to that time (which, given Alabama legal standards at the time, may mean that, at most, he did quite well). On top of all this, Pelham was much in demand with the ladies. He loved children and charmed his younger brother, Hugo, who worshiped him. Pelham, however, was doomed.

One day when he was twenty-two years old, Pelham drove the family horse and buggy to Taladega to visit a lady friend. This particular horse always turned right if not guided. Pelham and the lady spent a happy evening enhanced by delightful Taladega County brew. Returning home, Pelham fell asleep, and the horse, unguided, turned right—right into the mill pond. Pelham, the best swimmer in Clay County, never awoke.

This tragic event reinforced Daddy's lifelong fear and hatred of what he always referred to as "liquor." With his beloved brother's death and the humiliation he suffered over his father's propensity for the stuff, it is no wonder that he was always extremely uncomfortable around anyone who was drinking.

Orlando, a small, intense man, ten years older than Daddy, had a tremendous influence on him. He was a doctor and would drive all over the rural counties of Alabama on a motorcycle to deliver a baby, attend an old man who was dying, fight a fever, or calm the nerves of somebody suffering from a breakdown. Heedless of his own or his family's convenience, he made his calls whether the patients could pay or not. He literally sacrificed his life serving the people, rarely sleeping, eating only when he could, until finally this type of living burned him out. At forty-four, Orlando died of a disease of the arteries, "obliterative endarteritis." From that time on, "arteritis" was a word that plagued Daddy, one that he genuinely feared. This fear was not ungrounded, for temporal arteritis played its role in his own death.

When Hugo was about four years old, the family moved from Harlan to Ashland, a small farming community of approximately three hundred people. There, Fate opened a general store that fronted on the town square. Nearby, whenever the weather permitted, you could see men lounging about all four entrances to the courthouse playing checkers, or just sitting, spitting or talking and telling stories, unless court was in session, and a good trial was going on—then almost all of the loungers would go up to the courtroom to watch the drama. Hugo liked to hang around the square when he was a boy; and by the time he moved to Birmingham, he could whip anybody in the county at checkers—a skill that later proved useful when he ran for the Senate. He also became well-versed in courthouse lore. All the drama and excitement of the courtroom must have greatly impressed him and stimulated a love for the law that would never leave him.

There were some real characters in the courts in those days. The leading lawyer in Clay County was called Old Man Lackey. Old Man Lackey weighed three hundred pounds and used a specially built cane-bottomed chair to sit in, tilting it back and whittling while the case proceeded. His strong points were the opening statement and final argument. Old Man Lackey hated the effort of direct- and cross-examination of witnesses, but he had an eye for the jugular vein of the case. Daddy remembered a case where Old Man Lackey had been hired as special prosecutor to convict a Taladega man for the rape of a Clay County girl, because the parents of the girl were suspicious of the state prosecutor, he being from Taladega County. As usual, Old Man Lackey had a younger lawyer questioning the witnesses for him on direct- and cross-examination. The defense brought in witness after witness from Taladega County to attest to the character of the Taladega County rape suspect. When it came time for Old Man Lackey to argue, he dropped his knife and the piece of wood he was carving on, and stood up and faced the jury. Putting his hands on the rail of the jury box to support his enormous body, he said, "Folks. Ain't much to this case. This fella don't say much 'cept what a good fella he is over yonder in Taladega. Done brought plenty of Taladega County folks to swear to his cha-rac-ter too. Don't doubt it—don't doubt it at all. But, folks, I don't know about you, but I, fer one, am sick and tired of these Taladega boys coming over here to Clay County to raise all their hell. Now, you folks go on out there and send them Taladega boys that message." And the jury did.

Another lawyer Daddy would talk about was Charley Steed, who maintained an office above a millinery store run by a proper widow lady. Old Man Steed had a purple growth under his chin that dangled like a turkey gobbler's craw, and he could really holler out an argument, knees all bent and thumping the rail, his craw waggling under his chin impressively. He regarded himself as a "law man." He had two or three law books, and he would bring one of them to the courthouse to use if he got cornered. When this happened, he would open the book, search assiduously and always come up with a quote, right on the nose. The only remarkable thing was that for some reason the quote was always ungrammatical. When his opponent would try to check up on him, Old Man Steed would close the book and tell him disdainfully, "You get your own book if you gonna say what I say ain't in there."

One day the town awoke to find Old Man Steed and the milliner gone. No one in the county ever saw or heard of either of them again. But not long after they left, someone discovered that Old Man Steed had cut a trap door down into the millinery shop. Whenever the widow wanted to visit, all she had to do was put a box under the door, climb on top and knock. Old Man Steed would then pull her up into his office.

Besides playing checkers and watching the lawyers, my father swam at Hatchet Creek, and he and his pals played "burn-out," a game which determined who could stand the most pepper sauce on canned oysters. He also told me about his pet billy goat that really loved him, probably only because he fed him. He could ride that goat and get it to pull a cart, even though the billy goat had a mean streak and butted at everybody else. One night he butted Fate and that was the end of the pet goat.

Another thing that kept Hugo occupied was reading. He read everything he could get his hands on. His sister Ora, a schoolteacher, had supposedly been reading *Les Misérables* when he was born—hence the name Hugo—but most of the stuff she read was not of that quality. She provided Daddy with now obscure novels and poems and Civil War histories, and he himself got hold of detective stories. He loved Nick Carter stories and read all of them he could find. According to one of his boyhood friends, Hugo was off by himself reading much of the time, not really associating much with the other boys.

There was a school in town called Ashland College which was right across the street from the Blacks' home. Supported by both public and private funds, Ashland College not only awarded B.A. and B.S. degrees, but also included a grammar and high school. The town was proud of their school, which had students from all over the state. Daddy felt he got a pretty good education there, first with a Miss Lizzie Patterson, and then later at the hands of a teacher called Hiram Evans, who stimulated his curiosity about ancient Roman and Greek history. He never lost this love for the classics, and continued in later years to read all the Greek playwrights, in translation.

Physical problems caused him some worry as a boy. Once he secretly sent off for some freckle cream after reading an ad in a *Nick Carter* magazine. The ad promised that one application of this cream would obliterate all freckles. Sixty years later he told me: "I remember how it went now, Son—wipe on the cream, wipe off the freckles. Man, I rushed to the post office on fire at mail time every day. When it came, I hid it in the hayloft. Next day I did just what they said, I wiped on the cream. Trouble was when I wiped it off, I wiped off the skin on my face too. My mother tried to find out what had happened. My face looked like the skin of a rotten apple. But I wouldn't tell her."

"What happened with the freckles, Daddy?" I said.

"They stayed on till they were ready to go."

Then it was his weight. He felt he was so skinny that any virus that came along would be the end of him, and so he sent off for all sorts of weight nostrums. Of course, he eventually hit the stage where the problem reversed itself. Too much, not too little, weight became the problem.

It was hard for me to get a clear picture of what life was like for Daddy as a boy. I always had the feeling that he was controlling what he was passing on to me and the rest of his children about his early days in Clay County. He would never confide in me about his boyhood sufferings and joys the way he would talk about his professional life. Perhaps the explanation is that, by nature, he believed in keeping more things to himself than I do.

One thing he did talk a lot about was the kind of religion they practiced in Clay County. The church—that is, the Primitive Baptist Church which most everyone, including the Black family, belonged to—was the closest thing to "society" available. It nosed into everything, somewhat in the same way the old New England Puritan churches did. If someone got drunk, the congregation would "try" him and take a vote on whether or not to expel him. The only way such a person could reinstate himself was to become a mercy-begging penitent in front of the whole congregation. The same treatment awaited anyone accused of fornication, adultery or like sins. Crimes like murder they left to the courts so that the murderer could remain in the congregation if he wanted to pass judgment on others.

Another common practice was for members to stand up and witness to the Lord Jesus Christ when the spirit hit them. My father said he was always embarrassed when this happened to someone he liked or respected, and the person stood up and began to relate how the spirit hit him at a time when he had just committed adultery or fornication or was coming out of a drunken binge. "I would have felt much prouder of them if the spirit had hit them when they were full of the need to drink or for a woman." But most of all he was embarrassed when the spirit hit someone and demanded that he or she stand up and speak in tongues, or "gibberish," as Daddy said. "They claim the spirit is talking in his own language to them—moving them into ecstasy. Maybe so. Anyway, it's a harmless type of ecstasy. Doesn't hurt anybody else—maybe does them good. But, man, it's hard to sit there and listen to that stuff."

Although Hugo's mother was an intelligent woman and couldn't really be called a fundamentalist, she did insist that everyone go to church. Even as a boy, Hugo was very unhappy with these church practices, and he thought that the congregation inflicted punishment without justice. Public confessions and accusations were humiliating and embarrassing experiences that caused many people a lot of pain. It must have been especially hard for Hugo to witness his own father's expulsion and that of his Uncle Brack, John Breckenridge Toland, of whom he was very fond.

Uncle Brack was my grandmother's half-brother, and although he was built like all of us, of medium height and slight, that's where the resemblance stopped. He had fiery red hair, a fiery red beard and hair all over his body. Brack was fiercely independent, and kept body and soul together by scratching a bare living out of the hills of Clay County. He had one sweet time out of life. He loved to read; he loved children; he loved conversation; he loved to love; and he loved to get drunk. And everybody loved him—his mother and father, his brothers and sister; his children; his friends; and, ah, the ladies. When, as he put it, he was "filled up," he would leave his place out in the country and come into town to take up residence with his sister, Daddy's mother. He would tell her with a twinkle in his eye, "The moon's a'gonna shine tonight," and take off. That meant he was going out on a drunk and would come in about sunrise, soused to the gills. My father's mother never complained because such was his nature that alcohol always made this tender man even more tender.

Uncle Brack loved his oldest boy as he did his own life. One night when this boy was about twenty-one, he was at a dance where the brew flowed freely. A young lady coveted by a notorious mean drunk took to Uncle Brack's son. The man called Uncle Brack's son outside, whipped out a pistol, and murdered him in cold blood. The town got up a posse and went to Uncle Brack to get him to avenge his son's death. He stopped them, saying, "Let the law take its course, men, leave the murderer alone. Go on home." And the tears streamed down his cheeks.

In Clay County everyone predicted Uncle Brack would be dead by the age of forty because of his drinking, but I can remember going with Daddy to visit him when he was in his late eighties. Uncle Brack still had a red beard. He lived in a house where there was no electricity, no plumbing, no inside privy. When we got there, his wife, a woman in her fifties, was washing clothes in the creek. Uncle Brack seemed spry, but he had softened in the head. He refused to recognize Daddy, insisting I was Daddy, and we had a strange conversation. Uncle Brack talked to me, and Daddy talked to him. But he still twinkled, and we warmed in his presence, even if his head was out of whack. I like to think there is something of Uncle Brack in me. Although Daddy would not admit it because of Brack's drinking, I know he felt the same—he had a certain look on his face whenever he talked about him. It just was not the same as when he talked about Fate's drinking or the drinking of John Densler, Orlando's son, who died at age thirty-five and was the terrible example Daddy used to hold up to me and Sterling.

Maybe the church's expulsion of Fate and Brack contributed to Daddy's going back occasionally on his pronouncements to me that you should never poke fun by imitation. He would make fun of the church that expelled Fate and Brack by a hilarious imitation, singing through his nose songs like "How tedious and tasteless the hours when Jesus came into my life." He used to say to me:

"Son, if Jesus did something about those tedious and tasteless hours for those ladies, he has got to have some connection with the Lord. Passing the time for a lady past her prime sure required something special in Clay County in those days."

Hugo Finds His Profession

۔۔ۑ

Although Hugo had always planned to go to college, an incident occurred that prevented him from receiving even a high school diploma. One day Hugo's teenage sister, Daisy, was misbehaving and the teacher decided to mete out the usual punishment. He pulled up her skirts and started to give her a switching. Feeling that some lewdness was involved, Daddy sprang from his seat and ran across the street to tell his mother, who ordered him to go rescue Daisy. When he returned to the school, he grabbed the switch away from the teacher and broke it into pieces. Then he and the teacher pushed and shoved each other about. Daddy was very skinny—five ten and only a hundred and ten pounds—but he had a lot of fire in him and was able to put up a good fight. The outcome was that Hugo was expelled and couldn't graduate.

Such were the workings of the minds in the educational hierarchy of the State of Alabama in those days that you needed no college diploma, not even a high school diploma, to attend either law or medical school. Although

Daddy fondly remembered the courtroom scenes he had witnessed and frankly admitted that he loved to declaim before an audience at school or anywhere else, these feelings did not outweigh his desire to emulate his brother Orlando, who he thought contributed so much good to the community. So in 1903 Hugo entered Birmingham Medical School.

He performed brilliantly there. His high energy level and his natural aptitude for mathematical and scientific subjects enabled him to race ahead of the others, and in one year he obtained two years' credit. But the real reason for rushing ahead was that he wanted to get out. He did not like dismembering corpses and he could not stand the sight of blood or having to inflict physical pain even for the noble end of curing the sick. The smells around medical school affected his sensitive nose and almost made him retch.

In addition, the law still pulled on him. He told Orlando: "Lander, I can serve better as a lawyer. Maybe as a lawyer I can even serve a wider base of people than you can if I get into politics." So he left medical school after the first year and entered the University of Alabama law school, at Tuscaloosa. Law school there consisted of a very limited number of basic courses taught by two professors. To keep himself occupied he supplemented his schedule with courses in the School of Arts and Sciences at the university.

It was around this time that Daddy lost both his parents —his father a victim of cirrhosis of the liver, and his mother succumbing to pneumonia. I know his mother's death was a very tough thing for him, even though he never talked much about it to me. Fate was fifty-five and

Della fifty-seven when they died. At that time dying in one's fifties was not considered a premature death. There never was adequate medical care in Clay County and the diet was not the best. According to Barney Whatley, a lifelong friend of my father's, Fate and Della lived to a pretty ripe old age, because, if you thought of the average age of death in Clay County at that time, you'd realize it probably was around thirty-five. (Maybe that's why everyone over thirty-five was referred to as Old Man or Old Lady So-and-so).

In 1907, when he was twenty years old, Hugo graduated with high honors from the university law school, and automatically becoming a member of the Alabama bar and a full-fledged lawyer, he returned to Ashland to open an office. Even in the 1950's, when I practiced law in Alabama, there was only one lawyer in Clay County; in 1972 the lawyer population doubled—there were two instead of one. The business is just not there. If Daddy ever had any clients during the year he practiced in Clay County, he never told me about it. Fortunately for him, a happy accident occurred after he had "practiced" in Ashland for one year: his office burned down. This gave him the excuse to strike out on his own, and he moved to Birmingham, seventy-five miles from home.

At first he had to share an office with other lawyers, learning by example what to avoid in his profession. One of them he carefully described to me: "In the morning he came into his office. The newsboy had placed the paper on his desk. He would carefully carve off a piece of chewing tobacco and stick it in his jaw, and then he would get down to the business at hand. He would pick up that newspaper and go to work. He studied and studied it, stopping only to lean over and spit into his spittoon. He kept this up until noon, when he went out to lunch. Then he came back in from lunch and lay down for a nap. When he got up, he said, 'Hugo, here's a nickel. Would you go out and get me an afternoon paper?' Then he would read that until it was time to go home."

"How did he live, Daddy?"

"He took one-third of everything I and the other young lawyer boarders got from anybody who came into the office. 'Because,' the fella said, 'they come in to see me. It is my office.'"

At that time, Hugo lived and ate in a cheap boarding house. He had no money to get his "britches" pressed: "So I would just put them between the mattress and the springs very carefully every night before I went to bed, and I got me a pretty good press that way."

My father took any case he could get in those days, and there was one he especially enjoyed telling about—the case involving a boar. The animal had escaped from its fencing and got into a neighbor's yard, where it found a sow that permitted it to take liberties. When the issue of this union arrived, the owner of the boar claimed his share of the piglets, but the farmer who owned the sow felt that a trespasser boar was not entitled to any part of the issue. The boar's owner employed Daddy, who argued the case, winning half the litter for his client.

Hugo derived the steadiest part of his income in those days from writing reports on applicants for life insurance policies for fifty cents a case. This was hardly an encouraging situation for an ambitious young man, and he began to get discouraged with his position in Birmingham. Although the city was relatively young—incorporated in 1871—it had a highly stratified social structure, and a young man with no connections or "family" had a tough time fitting in. Because of this, Daddy considered moving to New York city, where it seemed there was a better chance of making money, or to Oklahoma Territory, where a young, aggressive man would fare well in politics.

Around about this time when things looked discouraging for Hugo, Barney Whatley, one of his boyhood friends, decided that he wanted to become a lawyer. In those days, a man could study under a lawyer, take the bar exam when he felt himself ready, and if he passed, become a member of the bar. Barney decided to study law with Daddy and proved a very fine pupil. After Barney passed the bar, the two formed what was to be the first of several partnerships Hugo would enter into in Birmingham. They got along beautifully. "That was an easy thing," Barney recalled. "All it took was doing whatever your daddy said. Now and then, though, I could get my way. I would just refer to our boyhood days in Clay County when he stole a citron thinking it was a watermelon, and I'd mutter, 'That's just what you'd expect from a fella don't know the difference between a citron and a watermelon.'"

In the beginning of their partnership, they were hard up for business, so they would get exposure by speaking at whatever events they could in the community. Barney said to me one day many years later: "We used to go to speakin's in those days to get business. Once we went to a meeting in East Lake where three people showed up. We didn't exactly know what to do, but they looked like they expected to hear from us. We used to memorize speeches for those things. That was before your daddy gained his great platform confidence and spontaneity, and your daddy had one speech he used at all speakin's, and he was always afraid to move off of it for fear he'd freeze. So your daddy stood up and looked squarely at those three people directly in front of him, snapped his head to the left and looked at empty space, snapped his head to the right and looked at empty space and pronounced in a serious, sober voice, 'As I look out over this vast sea of upturned faces—' "

Barney continued reminiscing: "I used to get all the business for the firm but, just as soon as I got it, your daddy would move in and take the client away. One day this black lady came in to see me, not him. As always, your daddy took over. Sometimes they didn't complain when he took over, but this one did. Before too long, she asked to see me alone, and she told me, 'Lawyer, I come to see you, not that little, old young sweet-faced lawyer. If you don't take my case back over, I'm goin' elsewhere. I believe in mean-faced lawyers. They the ones do you some good, an' you got the meanest-lookin' face any lawyer I ever seen.' "

This excellent partnership was abruptly terminated when the doctors informed Barney that he had TB, and sent him off to Colorado, where they thought the climate might add a few years to his life. It was only much later that Barney found out the "spots" on his lungs were nothing but the result of mechanical errors in the X-ray machine. In the meantime he had become a millionaire, specializing in mineral rights for companies out West. As long as he was single, Hugo went out to visit Barney every summer for a month and they got along famously, except for one sore spot—alcohol. All during their lives Daddy fussed at Barney for drinking liquor, and Barney fussed at Daddy for not drinking. When Daddy died, Barney could not resist saying to me, "Hugo, I always told your daddy he should drink more liquor. If he had, he would have outlived me and would have had to bear the sad news of my death."

After Barney left, Daddy's next partner was David J. Davis, a young man who had just graduated from Harvard law school. A man of delicate health and, according to Hugo, of saintly character, Daddy felt as close to David J. as he did to any man in those days. "There was never a time after I got to know David J. that I would not have entrusted him with my life, Son."

Hugo's first big break came when he appeared against William "Billy" Grubb before Circuit Judge A. O. Lane. Representing the steel company against which Hugo was trying to win a judgment, Billy Grubb had been practicing many years by this time and had the reputation of being the best corporate trial lawyer in Birmingham, and as such, the best pleader in town. The pleader had many tricks in those days, all of which were calculated to get a lawyer whose client had a meritorious case to make a mistake which would get the case dismissed. For instance, there was a rule that you could not work "a complete change of the parties." This meant that if the plaintiff's lawyer sued John Jones and it became evident during the trial that a certain Raymond Brown was really guilty, the lawyer could not then amend his complaint, but must start a new lawsuit. The real trick was to keep the plaintiff's lawyer in the dark about Raymond Brown until the statute of limitations had run out, then make the move after the deadline had passed for a new suit to be filed.

Another favorite ploy of a trial lawyer was the "join issue" game. When played by a reputable older lawyer against an easily awed younger lawyer, it often resulted in a case of merit going down the drain. In the "join issue" game, if you brought suit for a plaintiff who had proof that the defendant had negligently run a red light and injured the plaintiff, and the defendant pleaded an immaterial issue such as "The plaintiff drinks beer," and the plaintiff joined issue with the defendant denying that he drank beer, the plaintiff lost if it was proved that he had drunk even just a sip of beer. Laws such as these which enabled a smart lawyer to bypass the real right and wrong of a case were in effect in Alabama until a year or two ago.

On this particular occasion, my father made lifelong admirers of both Judge Lane and Billy Grubb by his pleading match with Billy. Billy tried all day to lead Daddy off on an immaterial plea, but Hugo each time would demur—i.e., plead, "So what?" On several occasions, Billy even had Judge Lane fooled, and Judge Lane overruled Hugo's demurrer. Hugo, however, said he would stand on his demurrer and would allow Billy to take a judgment against his client for failing to join issue after a demurrer overruled, and then Hugo would appeal. Hugo repeated his arguments again for Judge Lane in the teeth of Bill's attempts to stop him by every insult imaginable; and each time my father convinced Judge Lane that if he persisted in refusing the demurrer, he would most certainly be reversed. This went on all day until Judge Lane finally said, "Billy, you better get down to the merits. This young fellow is not going to bite on any of that stuff."

"I guess you're right, Judge," Billy said.

Deeply impressed by his performance, Billy offered Hugo a partnership in his firm. But Daddy was not about to give up his independence and devote his legal career to the defense of the special interests, so he politely declined. He knew it was possible to make just as much money, if not more, defending injured people who didn't have any money with a contingent fee contract.

Not long afterward, Judge Lane called Hugo to his office. "Hugo," he said, "I have the right to appoint the judge of the police court of Birmingham. I want to change the image over there. I need a young fellow with exceptional ability, and strength of character too, in that job, and I want you to take it."

Hugo accepted, with the understanding that he could still continue with his own law practice. He was on his way.

By this time, Daddy had begun to circulate around town as only a single man driven by ambition can afford to do. A lot of the restless energy that boiled in him was the result of a hyperthyroid condition. He could neither sleep well nor keep his mind from racing, and he no sooner finished one task than he started looking for another. It wasn't until he was in his forties that he had a goiter operation to correct this condition, but up until then he directed this excess energy toward advancing his career, thus turning a handicap into an advantage.

The last fifteen years or so of his life he also gave himself testosterone shots, which he told me he took as a substitute for part of his thyroid shots.

I accused him: "You're taking those for another reason, Daddy."

"I don't need them for that reason, Son."

"Maybe not. But you're afraid you do."

"That could be so, Son. But the doctors prescribe it."

"Who tells them what's needed?" I said—answering my own question with "You do, Daddy."

Hugo joined practically every organization a man could belong to, except those which would not allow dual membership, or those, such as the "elite" Kiwanis Club, who would not have him because of his background. As a member of the Masons (ultimately becoming a 33rd degree Mason), Woodmen of the World, Redmen, Civitan Club, Eagles, Elks and Dokies, he demonstrated a remarkable memory by mastering the complicated rituals of these and other organizations. Somehow, in spite of his busy schedule, he found time to recruit one thousand members for the Knights of Pythias, a feat that made his lodge extremely proud of him.

Another project he undertook was to teach the Baraca class for adults at the Sunday School of the First Baptist Church in Birmingham, which he continued to do for over twenty years. When he read from the Bible and then interpreted the passage, he made a deep impression on all who listened. He was in effect a preacher without a cloth, sometimes attracting as many as a thousand people to his classes. In many of the sermons delivered to working people, they were told not to worry about the bad conditions today because there was the Promised Land tomorrow, but Hugo's approach was different and he was able to really inspire. I've had people come up to me years later and tell me how much they got out of my father's talks.

A first-rate checkers player, he became popular at firehouses where he would take on the local champion. The policemen in town liked him well enough to make him the lawyer for their fraternal organization. He made all sorts of friends, rarely turning down a dinner invitation, and as a result his practice began to flourish. One case I remember his telling me about involved a man—whom I shall call Jud Sims—who later became one of the hardest workers in Hugo's Senate campaigns.

Jud ran a drugstore in a little town adjoining Birmingham called Pratt City. At that time local toughs roamed about demanding tribute from each merchant, what in these days would be called protection money. Because the police would do nothing to stop these toughs, Jud came to Hugo and asked whether it would be legal for him to kill if they tried to carry out their threats. My father went out to the area with Jud Sims and confronted two of these men, who denied any knowledge of tributes or threats. Afterward, Jud received anonymous letters describing what would happen to him if he did not comply with their demands.

In the meantime Daddy had devised a plan that would shed light on the truth of the situation if something happened to Jud or to the toughs at Jud's hands. Soon after the confrontation, Hugo said to Jud, "Let's go to the bank and rent us a safe deposit box. We'll take two fellas from the bank with us and go down and put these anonymous letters in the box; the two bank fellas will record and keep the dates; then we'll leave the key to the box with these fellas at the bank. Also, I want you to date and write a letter to one of the fellas at the bank every time the bullies threaten you, and we'll deposit that in the box at the bank using the same procedure."

Thereafter, each time the bullies came to call, Jud followed this plan. "I also had Jud report the incident to the police every time the bullies came back, making sure it was written down on the blotter. Then just to make sure, I went out and looked at the police blotter myself to see the calls were there. They were."

Finally the toughs realized they weren't going to get any money out of Jud, so one day they returned to the drugstore and began attacking him with a knife and club. Jud reached down behind the counter, brought out a rifle and shot them both dead on the spot.

The county solicitor charged Jud with first-degree murder. Hugo pleaded self-defense in Jud's behalf, and it took the jury only about five minutes to decide to acquit him.

Hugo's success was becoming too much for David J. Davis. They were dividing all their income evenly, and although Hugo was willing to allow that to continue forever, David J. said his conscience was bothering him about taking as much as Hugo, because he just could not bring in the same amount of business or produce as much when it got there. My father begged him not to break up the partnership, but he was determined. David J. could not allow himself to take his share, and yet he could not be in a partnership on the basis of anything less than even earnings. Even though the partnership was dissolved, David J. remained my father's lawyer until many years later when he was appointed a United States district judge on Hugo's recommendation. "So far as I was concerned," my father said, "there just was nobody else in contention."

Now that Hugo had established a secure foothold in the relatively closed society of Birmingham, he felt less pressured by financial concerns and was eager to begin satisfying his political ambitions.

Politics and
a Brief Taste of
Military Glory

In 1914, Daddy resigned from police court and decided to make his first political move by running for the office of county solicitor. At that time the office of county solicitor was occupied by a very popular man from a famous Alabama political family, Harrington P. Heflin. One method Hugo used in his campaign was to circulate petitions all over Jefferson County demanding that Hugo Black be elected county solicitor. Lodge brothers, members of his Sunday School class, his clients, policemen and firemen all signed and distributed them everywhere until there appeared to be a veritable grass-roots demand for Hugo Black. Not to be outdone, Harrington Heflin circulated his own petitions demanding that he be retained as county solicitor, and practically everyone who signed Hugo's petition signed Mr. Heflin's.

Hugo then countered by coming up with an issue. Birmingham in those days was plagued by pickpockets. Each time the police caught one and charged him, he promptly made bail and was never seen again. There apparently was some sort of ring, which maintained a collective treasury to make bond for any member who got caught, and as a result they couldn't care less about getting arrested. Daddy deplored this situation and promised that he would put an end to it if elected.

Election Day came, and Hugo's tireless campaigning in every nook and cranny of Jefferson County paid off. Hugo edged past Harrington and won. True to his pledge, he made sure that the next pickpocket who was arrested had to put up a bond that was extraordinarily high. He successfully fought off charges that the bond was excessive by explaining that a lesser bond would not ensure that the pickpocket would show up for trial. And sure enough, not too long after he was elected, the pickpocket ring deserted Birmingham. Hugo Black had cured the pickpocket plague, a fact he was not shy about reporting.

According to Mr. Ben Ray, who at that time was one of my father's assistants, a great backlog of cases had accumulated under Mr. Heflin, and Hugo—with his tremendous energy—set out to whittle it down. As well as trying cases himself, he brought in judges from all over the state, until the load was reduced to manageable proportions.

Mr. Ben told me that Daddy originated a policy of not trying anyone on the basis of a confession alone, since his suspicions of police brutality in extorting confessions had been confirmed by a special grand jury inquiry that he had instigated. He demanded that there be strong independent evidence corroborating the confession before he would agree to proceed. According to Mr. Ben, "If there was the slightest taint on the confession he would not use it. In that case, he demanded that the evidence independent of the confession be sufficient to convict without reference to the confession at all."

Mr. Ben also said: "Hugo would not let us try the case if he thought our witnesses were lying. He put them through the third degree in certain types of cases before he would go ahead. In rape cases, incest, that type of stuff, Hugo thought there was a good chance that the prosecution witness might be lying. Labor cases, the same way. But if he thought the witnesses were telling the truth, he would prosecute those kind of cases all-out same as in any other case."

Another policy Daddy originated that cost him on his won-and-lost record concerned race. In those days the juries in Birmingham were all-white. The unwritten law for a criminal jury trial lawyer said that you could never convict a white man for an offense against a black person; you could never convict a black man for an offense against a black person, "they were just bein' niggers"; and you could always convict a black man for an offense against a white person. According to Mr. Ben, Hugo refused to go by these customs. When I talked to Mr. Ben, he still used the crude language of the old days: "Hugo just felt that the niggers out in their quarter were entitled to enjoy the same peace and freedom from bullyin' that the white people are, and he aimed to do somethin'. I tell you somethin' too—Hugo got some of 'em. Some of 'em got away, but he got some. He just used the argument that the law owed those kinda people the same kinda peace it owed somebody over on the South Side.

"If Hugo didn't believe the white man who wanted to charge a nigger, Hugo just would see to it that no indictment or information came out, that's all. Maybe the jury would have convicted, but Hugo never gave 'em the chance. He didn't make any big deal out of it. Just nothin' ever happened."

"How about convicting a white man for an offense against a black person?"

"Well now, I can't remember that ever happened. But let me ask you somethin'. It's 1958—can you see that happenin' today?"

I had to answer, "No, sir."

Hugo not only got some good administrative experience, but he also packed a lot of trial experience into those few years, and learned a good deal about a community's unwritten laws. One time he attempted to convict a man who had brutally murdered his wife's lover on a corner of downtown Birmingham. The defendant was acquitted. Later a member of the jury told him what they all felt: "When a fella goes to fooling around with another man's wife, he runs the risk of getting killed if he gets caught, that's all there is to it."

Hugo also learned that there was no sense in trying to convict a striker who had been charged with assault and battery for hitting a non-striker on the head for crossing the picket line. There would always be somebody on the jury who believed that nobody had the right to cross a picket line during a strike, and invariably the jury would be hung.

Another unwritten law that Daddy learned was that you were never going to recover for a lady who appeared in court displaying diamonds and furs, even if the defendant had negligently rammed her car and seriously injured her. The only chance you had to recover for her was to make her dress very modestly.

One thing that Hugo really cracked down on was liquor. Alabama was a prohibition state at that time, but a flourishing "near beer" industry had grown up, because it was impossible to convict for the sale of beer without proof beyond a reasonable doubt by a chemical analysis that the beer had enough alcohol in it to be intoxicating. Alabama then passed a law making it an offense to sell or possess beer or any liquid that looked like or tasted like beer. The brewers hired a prominent Birmingham lawyer, Forney Johnston, to challenge the constitutionality of the law under the due process clause of the Fourteenth Amendment. Hugo defended the law successfully and Mr. Johnston's petition for injunction was dismissed.

Mr. Johnston was a formidable man who did not easily take defeat. He readily became a staunch ally of Joe Tate, the circuit solicitor who was determined to challenge the constitutionality of the state law under which the job of county solicitor was created. Because the jurisdictions of circuit solicitor and county solicitor were frequently the same in Jefferson County, there was a good chance that the men, who did not like the way Hugo was hurting their special interests, could attack his authority. After a series of complicated legal maneuvers by Tate and Johnston, the Alabama Supreme Court finally decided that Hugo would be forced to use assistants appointed by Joe Tate. Rather than have his job undermined in this way, Hugo resigned as county solicitor.

After the United States entered World War I, Daddy—who was then thirty-one—decided to join the Army, and in the spring of 1917, was assigned to the Field Artillery Division. Although he wanted to go overseas—thinking it might be a strike against him in postwar politics if he couldn't join the Veterans of Foreign Wars—he remained in the States, serving to train men in California and Fort Sill in Oklahoma.

Except for using his Army career as a source of funny stories, Daddy never said too much about this period of his life. He hated wars; before the United States entered that war, he supported the neutrality stance of William Jennings Bryan, and later he opposed both the Korean and Vietnam wars. Despite his great interest in history, he was never interested in military tactics, and in contrast to my maternal grandfather, he never discussed Civil War strategies with me. When he talked about Caesar's conquests, he always pointed out to me that Caesar forgave some of his enemies, and he thought this might be one of the reasons for his success.

While he was a captain at Fort Sill, he acquired one of the best stories he used to tell on himself. One day, his commander assigned him to take his company out and maneuver it around. Hugo had religiously learned the hand signals of command in anticipation of this day. But he said that once the maneuver began, it became apparent that he had somehow offended the sergeant who assigned the horses.

"Son," he said to me, "I've thought and thought and I can't figure what wrong I did that sergeant. But it had to be something because he gave me an unmanageable horse, a general horse who liked to command. I was on trial, and my men were watching me carefully. Just as soon as I got on him, the horse broke into a gallop for the woods. I gave the gallop sign to my men and gave out with a rebel yell as if this were my plan, and they followed. He felt like he was going to go to the right, and I gave the right-turn signal and hollered 'Hooooo-ooooo,' and down through the woods we went helter-skelter in a roaring gallop. Then I got the feeling that he was going to double back. So I gave the double-back signal and let out another rebel yell. By this time, my hat was off my head and hanging on the strap around my neck. I looked back, and my men were following, some of them whipping their horses to keep up. We kept going at this wild pace for a few more minutes when I felt my horse getting tired. All of a sudden he slowed to a canter and started for home, and I gave the appropriate signals. The horse sighed. I sighed. And then we were back at the horse barn. I gave the dismount signal and got off as quick as I could.

"A private came up to me and said, 'Captain Black, I feel we are ready to ride right in under enemy fire tomorrow, set up, and blast 'em. You are a bold and daring captain. I am glad I have the chance to serve under you.'

"I saluted and said, 'Be off, sir.' But from then on, my men were convinced that I was a daring commander and one of the finest horsemen in the Army."

While he was in the Army, he also met and served under a man whom I will call General H. Lee Randolph, who would become his law partner after the war. In the Army, the General was considered—by himself as well as others—a mathematical genius. "You measure the intelligence of a man," he used to say, "by the level of abstraction he is capable of reaching, and I have always been able to ascend to the highest level and sustain thoughts on that level for a considerable period of time."

The General was a fine figure of a man—a fact he was well aware of. "In those days, I had a very difficult decision to make every evening. For some reason, every young lady in the area of camp wanted me. And it was very hard for me to select one and hurt the feelings of the others," said he.

Back in the 1950's the General and I would talk for hours at a time as he sipped eight or nine drinks before lunch at Joy Young's restaurant in Birmingham. He always spoke in the deep, resonant voice and measured tones of a Shakespearean actor; my father said he spoke the same way in the Army. "To what did you attribute this fascination, General? Was it your appearance or your manner?"

"I don't think it was either, Hugo, really. I think it was my reputation for performance. My prowess in the bedroom was legendary, as, of course, it still is to a lesser extent."

"How did you become so friendly with Daddy?"

"He was my protégé. He is, of course, as you know, quite brilliant in his own right. We used to converse mathematically, which all the men considered a feat. Of course, mathematics is just language, and two who know the language can converse just as you and I are doing here now."

"I wouldn't know, General. Did Daddy go on any of these adventures at night with you?"

"As you are aware, your father's health has always been rather delicate. Mine, on the other hand, has been robust. He must sleep. I never need sleep. You also know that your father is very much afraid of liquor and has stayed away from it. I, on the other hand, have always imbibed, because liquor has little effect on me in any way, and it has always been that way. So your father and I in the main traveled different roads at night."

The General was a man of vast contradictions. During his dry spells back in the fifties he would tell me, "What gives you the idea I drink? I have never been a drinker."

Sometimes the General would tell me, "Hugo, I don't suppose one man has ever been more loyal to his wife than have I. I have been married, lo, these thirty-odd years, and never have I been disloyal with another woman." (He did indeed raise a remarkably fine family with his charming wife.)

Then later I saw him after he had been in the hospital, and said, "Have you recovered, General?"

"Several days ago. But I started topping this young nurse, and we extended my hospital stay. Never in the history of this world has one man topped as many women as I have. They have not been able to leave me alone, and I have not had the strength to resist them."

Or he would say, "I have never missed an income tax payment."

Then he would say, "You can't tolerate anything from these income tax people. When they come up and bother me and say, 'You have filed your income tax return but paid nothing,' I just tell them, 'Do what you will, I have nothing.' They go away and don't come back, because they know I will pay when and if I can."

Daddy would not say much about the General in the Army. But he did confirm that the General had been considered a mathematical genius and, in actuality, probably was. The picture I got of him was of a man of tremendous talent and equally monumental appetite, the two constantly striving against each other, making him at times a quite noble character.

"There is absolutely no question about his intellectual

prowess, Son," my father said. "The words flow from him precisely and accurately. His gift for expression is extraordinary. He can analyze, synthesize and reason brilliantly. When he is feeling all right, he has a deep well of energy and the stamina of a bull. It was these qualities that convinced me he would make a valuable partner. I knew about his pomposity, his conceit and his instability when I went into partnership with him, but I believed he would mature out of it."

When Daddy and the General came out of the Army, they formed the partnership of Black and Randolph. If Judge C.B. Smith is to be believed, the General had his own reasons for moving to Alabama with Hugo. Judge C.B. said to me that one day the General asked him, "C.B., do you know why I moved to Birmingham from Georgia?" The judge said no. "Well, I got out the books and I found that Georgia had had a Supreme Court justice since Alabama, and I would have a better chance if I came from Alabama rather than from Georgia." Judge C.B. then commented on this statement to me: "He wasn't too far off after all. His partner made it."

Hugo Becomes
a Family Man

A few weeks before Armistice Day, November 11, 1918, Hugo was discharged from the Army. He returned to Birmingham, where he began working very hard to build up his law practice. But for all his hard-nosed sense of reality, Daddy had a romantic streak in him. Before going into the Army, he had fallen in love with a girl whose parents were Orthodox Jews. They had agreed to marry, but when her parents found out, Daddy was not allowed to ever see her again because he was not of her faith. Now, getting on into his thirties, he was to fall victim to something he really believed in, love at first sight.

One day as he was driving down Niazuma Avenue, a posh residential section of the South Side, Hugo saw a woman talking with a friend in front of no. 1313. Daddy later told me, "I determined right then and there that I would marry that girl. There was something about the way she walked, something about the way she listened and smiled and replied to what the other girl was saying. Of course, she looked good physically, but it was more than that. She just seemed to have a sweet nobility about her. She just seemed to reflect a spiritual quality."

As usual, Daddy did not procrastinate. He went right to work inquiring about who she was. It turned out that she was one of the Foster girls, and since the oldest one, Josephine, had brown hair, and the youngest, Virginia, red hair, Hugo knew he had seen Josephine Foster, and immediately began to maneuver for an introduction. In short order, Daddy had that introduction and his first date with Mama.

Josephine was the second child of Dr. Sterling J. Foster and Anne "Nana" Foster. Nana's father, Colonel Josiah Patterson, had been a Confederate war hero, who reputedly had made a dramatic escape from the Yankees by leaping off a horse over the railing of a bridge into a roiling, boiling stream. Largely on the basis of this feat, Colonel Patterson later served several terms as a very conservative member of the U.S. Congress. Nana's brother, Malcolm Patterson, followed in his father's footsteps and served two terms as a very conservative governor of the State of Tennessee.

When Daddy began keeping company with Mama, she was barely twenty-one and he was thirty-four. Mama had attended the public schools in Birmingham and then gone off to Virginia to Sweet Briar Academy, which, in those days, was a bridge between high school and Sweet Briar College, where young ladies of the South could learn all the secrets of genteel Southern womanhood. While at Sweet Briar, Mama contracted a mild rheumatic fever which affected her heart permanently. When the First World War broke out, Mama enlisted in the Navy as a Yeomanette, and was stationed in New York City doing clerical work.

Josephine's parents shamelessly favored her over her brother, Sterling, and sister, Virginia, and at the same time her brother and sister shamelessly favored her over each other and over their parents. In kindergarten and grammar school, she was the little girl who got all the notes and valentines from the boys, yet the girls always referred to her as their best friend. When she grew old enough to have dates, the boys pursued her relentlessly. The diary she kept in New York while she was a Yeomanette shows that she had an average of three dates a day. But she never had any problems with improper advances either in New York or Birmingham, because all of her dates seemed to revere her and most certainly had marriage in mind.

Josephine's appeal came not from her physical appearance—although that was pleasant enough—but from something inside her. Mama had brown hair when Hugo first knew her, but, even then, there was a white hair or two among the brown. For most of her life with Daddy, she had a radiant head of prematurely white-gray hair that set off her playful, sky-blue eyes in striking contrast. Her complexion was slightly marred by a few scars which were the result of very serious adolescent acne, and she had thick ankles and heavy calves. She was also rather full-hipped, and her thighs were dappled like buttermilk. Although her breasts were well-proportioned, they were small, definitely not the kind that made men stare with bulging eyes when she walked by.

Despite this, no beautiful woman had a chance with any man in whom Josephine had the slightest interest. Something about her captivated you and made you adore her, no matter whether you were male or female, gas station attendant or President of the United States. She was a listener, and, as she listened, she fastened her sky-blue eyes on you and made you feel that what you were pouring out was all that really mattered in the world to her. When you finished talking with her, you felt purged of what had been bothering you, and left with a real sense of self-worth.

Josephine was not stricken with love for Hugo at the very beginning. At the time, she had at least two other suitors who were very intent on winning her hand, and she might have been a little wary of him at first, since he was considered to be a common, crude man—even communistic—and everyone warned Mama that she was betraying her class by going out with him. But as Mama later told me, "I had never seen any man before with so much confidence. He assumed that I was fated to marry him and that everybody else was out of the picture. He was like an irresistible force; he just kept coming at me. Everyone in that false society we lived in felt he was common, yet they all conceded that he had no equal at his business, that he was supreme among the lawyers. I had never been exposed to a mind like his. And, of course, he had the charm of a much older man who still has his youthful appearance; he seemed so sophisticated yet somehow so youthful. He had big plans and no doubt that he would achieve them. Although many men had been in love with me before, nobody ever looked at me with such total adoration."

Hugo always used to say, "If I have accomplished anything real in this world, it was talking your mother into marrying me. I don't know how I did it."

It took a good year of energetic courting for Josephine to finally make up her mind. They were married on February 23, 1921, a few days before Hugo turned thirty-five.

Before long there were two other males in the household vying for Josephine's attention—I came along on April 29, 1922, and Sterling on September 12, 1924. I was not the well-behaved model child my father had been when he was a boy.

When I was very young I would often hear my grandparents telling people with a tone of pride and a chuckle, "That boy is the most high-spirited boy anybody ever saw. He has really got a high temper. Maybe it's the little bit of red in his hair." After I heard them say this, I really turned that temper loose. I learned how to kick at my nurses, stomp on their toes, yell at them, throw things, and otherwise live up to what everyone would expect from that red-haired, temperamental child.

Less enamored of my high spirits than were my grandparents, my nurse finally reached the breaking point when I stomped on her toe as she was trying to get me to take a bath. She screamed, and then slammed me up against the tub—the result was a blood-gushing cut over my right eye.

After we got back from the doctor, Mama in her gentle way was trying to crank herself up to fire my nurse when Daddy walked in.

"Good Lord," he said, looking at my bandaged head. "What happened to Hugo?"

"Lou threw him up against the bathtub," Mama said.

Lou stood there crying. Daddy probably could tell something by my look because he didn't seem too angry with her. "What happened, Lou?" he asked.

"I was just trying to give the boy a bath. He came stomping on my feet and I threw him upside the tub. I'm real sorry, Mr. Black."

He looked down at me. "Did you do that, Son?"

Then I started crying and said, "I'm sorry, Daddy, but I have this high temper and I just couldn't help it."

"Lou, you fix me some dinner," he said. Then he led me to the bathroom and pulled down my pants and spanked me good. When he got through he said, "Son, don't you ever let me hear talk about any high temper again. Every fool in this world is born with a high temper. It's nothing to be proud of. Nobody is born with one any worse than anybody else's. You got to learn to control it. Don't you ever again boast around about any fool high temper." I still have a scar over my right eye to remind me of this lesson.

Mary Marble, our maid, protected me and Sterling; like a mother hen, she considered us her boys. Although she would fight anybody who said anything against either of us, she knew how to make us behave by telling us about the Sack Man: "He carries a big old burlap sack that he puts bad little boys in. Look there—he there, you boys better do right." In those days there was always an old black man with a burlap sack scavenging around in Birmingham, so the threat meant something awful to us.

Mary believed in the Lord Jesus Christ, and she taught me and Sterling about the Bible. I remember one line she always made us repeat: "Jesus wept." At the time we didn't know what it meant, but when we quoted it, tears would flow from under her gold-rimmed glasses.

Life to Mary was no laughing matter. Something was always wrong, and she was in a perpetual state of unhappiness, complaining all the time. Finally, Mama simply could not stand the gloom anymore and she got Daddy to let Mary go.

At first Daddy's standard punishment was spanking, but I broke him of that one day when I cried long and loud enough to wear him out. After that, he punished my brother and me with confinement to our bedroom or the yard. When Mama could not get us to eat, he would grab hold of the spoon and demand, "Open up." When we did, he would shovel down a spoonful. But he stopped when my "sensitive stomach" just could not take any more food, and "Open up" produced nothing but retching.

He also had the idea that I had to be "purged" every so often with calomel pills and castor oil.

"Open up," he'd say.

"Daddy, the stuff makes me sick. I don't want to take it anymore."

"You *will* take it."

But when a brilliant man makes this kind of decision, even a wee child's mind can figure out a way to frustrate him. From then on, whenever he gave me calomel or castor oil, I simply retched.

He saved face by saying, "Hugo is allergic to that stuff," and never tried the purge treatment on any of us after that. But it did not stop his use of force against his children; it only tempered it. He still had a long way to go.

Trial
Lawyer

When Daddy was practicing law in Birmingham, the city was dominated by the U. S. Steel Corporation through a subsidiary, the Tennessee Coal, Iron and Railroad Company (TCI). The rich deposits of coal and ore in the hills surrounding the town were mined by underpaid workers and prisoners, who had been rented by the state to certain companies and who suffered brutal treatment. There were also many industrial workers who worked grueling twelve-hour shifts in the steel mills with a twenty-four-hour swing shift every two weeks. As could be expected with the terrible working conditions, there were many industrial accidents, and it was not uncommon for workers to lose fingers and toes or suffer horrible deaths.

Since there was no workman's compensation, Hugo usually represented plaintiffs who had been injured, taking them on a contingent-fee contract in which he would get a percentage of the judgment if he won and nothing if he lost. His business principally came from other contingent-fee lawyers who wanted him to try the case before a jury so that their clients would recover more. As a leader of the plaintiff's bar, he helped ensure the principle that a prisoner who was working in a mine under the convict-leasing system had a right of action against the company, and he himself pleaded for two black prisoners. Many of the prisoners were blacks who had been arrested for minor offenses under a corrupt fee system (abolished in 1915) that made many law officers very rich; I would say that this convict-leasing system was really nothing better than a disguised form of slavery.

Now and then Hugo would take a case for an insurance company or other establishment corporation, but only on his own terms—and they were tough. He represented one insurance company on a regular basis, but made them give him absolute discretion as to which cases would be tried and which settled. In his last full year of practice (1925), his income reached $80,000 a year, which for those days was fabulous money.

Hugo also represented unions, even though a man called White Gibson was their principal attorney. Workers needed these unions to protect them from being exploited not only by the low pay, long hours and terrible living conditions, but also from such things as the care they received in TCI's company hospital. The doctors there were employed by TCI, and they would appraise the workers' injuries in such a way that the company would have to pay only a minimum compensation. Some of the doctors even went so far as to develop a thesis that coal dust was beneficial because it protected the lungs. It wasn't until 1949, when I moved to Birmingham, that a worker could get compensation for having developed silicosis in the mines.

There were constant attempts by the unions to organize, but these efforts invariably met with violence. It was a well-known fact that the coal industry hired security employees who circulated around the company towns, and if they found someone agitating for unionization, he might very well wind up dead. This, of course, did nothing but stir up the bitterness and hatred of the people who lived in the dingy hovels the company provided. Indeed, recognizing how resentful the workers must have felt toward the well-off people in the town, the Supreme Court of Alabama made it an automatic ground for a mistrial for a lawyer to work into his argument a reference to the elegant South Side of Birmingham in the hope that he could stir up the animosity of the jury.

I learned most of what I know about my father as a trial lawyer from the judges and lawyers who were around in his day and who still worked there when I myself practiced law in Birmingham. No matter how much one of them might have disliked Hugo, everyone conceded that he was practically unbeatable in the courtroom. "Old Ego [as his enemies called him] had a way in there. You can't take that away from him."

Judge Clarence Mullins, who was on the United States District Court when I practiced in Birmingham, greatly admired him but confessed that he sometimes called him "Ego" too. He remembered the day that he and a friend were standing outside the Frank Nelson Building talking when Ego emerged on the fly. Cordial greetings were exchanged, and then, as Hugo continued on his way Clarence's friend commented, "Look at the little sonofabitch. He thinks he is goin' to be President of the United States." Clarence Mullins replied, "You know the little sonofabitch just might."

J. K. "Jake" Taylor, who once practiced with Daddy, always prided himself on his selection of juries. He would see that each prospective juror answered a lot of questions calculated to find out whether he leaned toward privilege and power or the little man—questions about the part of town he had lived in, where he bought his clothes, his church preferences and employment history, his acquaintance with parties involved and known witnesses, and so forth.

One day Jake came up to me in the hall of the courthouse while I was talking to another lawyer and said, "I watched you striking a jury the other day. All you said was, 'I'll take the jury in the box.' That's dangerous stuff."

"Not in that case," I said.

"Damn you, boy," he said, "you gettin' bad as your Daddy. He's only man I ever saw didn't give a damn who was on the jury—figured he would get 'em anyway, no matter who they was. Always would snap, 'I'll take the jury in the box,' and turn around and smile at 'em. Cockiest lawyer ever I seen."

The other lawyer I had been talking to, Mr. George Yancy, who at seventy-five was still trying cases, broke in and said, "Now, Jake, he didn't do that out of cockiness at all. He did it because he knew it would impress the jury—make 'em think his case was so good he didn't need to worry who was on the jury. He'd do it with his worst case, just like his good ones. It generally worked for him too. Made each juror on the box feel Hugo had confidence in him to do the right."

"Hell of a gamble," said Jake.

"Hugo gambled in a trial," said Mr. Yancy, "and for him most always it worked out. It's his judgment. It's damn near uncanny."

Mr. Yancy went on to tell me that Daddy's gambling enabled him to get more out of witnesses hostile to his case than anyone had a legitimate right to expect:

"Know what everybody says is the first rule of cross-examination? Don't ask a question unless you know first what answer you're gonna get. Your Daddy never paid any attention to that. Damn, Hugo could get more out of witnesses by bluffing than anybody I ever saw. Never lied. Just took stabs and hit the heart. Could see what you or your witness was scared of and, without telling you he had it, make you believe he did have it when he might not. He could do one hell of a lot with a blank piece of paper. I've tried, but can't bring it off. It's his facial expressions much as anything.

"Another thing—he'll find out some enemy of the witness who *could* be in a position to witness the same thing. Without saying it, he'll make your witness believe the enemy was going to come up and testify—and then your witness would start hedging and the sonofabitch had you."

"Good as he was in cross-examination," Judge C.B. Smith told me once, "that wasn't his strongest point. It was the final argument. You go through all the things in the book supposed to be so poisonous you can't say them. Well, Hugo could get 'em all in without actually saying 'em. He could mimic someone by using a raised eyebrow or a certain posture or inflection of his voice.

"Catch him on some point and he's like a cat. Always lands on his feet—cocky as ever—change the whole theory of his case and wonder why he hadn't thought of the new theory before.

"He'd ruin everybody. I remember a streak Borden Burr

was riding. Didn't lose one for twenty, twenty-five cases, then he met up with Hugo. Borden'd bulldoze. Near always could get away with it. He'd laugh or whistle when the other fella'd score a good one on cross-examination. Well, this time he caught Hugo with a case Hugo wished he'd never taken. Hugo tried and tried to settle, but Borden wouldn't pay him a dime. Hugo's man had a leg off, but if the case had been non-jury I would have had to say it was his fault. Went to work drunk and the mine car ran over him. Well, old Hugo played it cautious. He proved just enough for it to go to the jury. Borden was a bad enough laugher and whistler when the other fella had a good case, but when the other side had a bad one, Borden went wild. Everything Hugo'd say, Borden would cackle and whistle, saying what a silly case he had. Hugo just sat there, lips pressed together, putting his fingers together at the tips like he did when he was holding himself in, kinda looking at the ceiling.

"Borden's closing was just brilliant. I didn't see how Hugo could do anything after that, but he did. He walked up there, and he called his client up there before the jury with him, his client on crutches, his left pants leg empty to the hips—a really fine-looking young man with his wife and three little children sitting in the gallery so's the jury could see them.

" 'Gentlemen,' Hugo said, 'we have all been treated to a grand performance. Neither Fatty Arbuckle nor Charlie Chaplin could have given us a better show. Mr. Burr's a comic genius. But the line between the comic and what the poets call sadistic is a slim one. Maybe Mr. Burr knows the difference. But look here, gentlemen, look here.'

"He pulled out the empty pants leg and tears glistened on his cheeks.

" 'That's not funny to me. Not funny at all. But did you hear Mr. Burr? He laughed and cackled all over this court-room.'

" 'Go on, son, you can sit down now,' Hugo said to his client. 'Let me help you.' When he got his client seated, he walked back before the judge and said, " 'Yes, to Mr. Burr it was the laugh of the century. And he was having so much fun at the expense of this young husband and father that he just couldn't be courteous. He got to whis-tling when I got to questioning or trying to make a point. Just wouldn't let us put our case in. Well, gentlemen, do you think all this would happen if they didn't know what they owe this fine young husband and father? I've showed you by the actual tables how long he's got to live without his leg. You know what he earned—you know what they owe him. Go out there and teach Mr. Burr that losing a leg is a crying, not a laughing, matter. That losing a leg is not something to whistle or sing about—it's a matter for justice. Teach Mr. Burr and his client what it means to chew off a man's leg for profit.'

"When Hugo got through, some of 'em were crying. The jury came back with one of the biggest verdicts they ever returned up to that time. You'd have thought it would'a made Borden stop all that whistling and laughing but it didn't. He's still doing it."

Judge Smith sat musing for a while, then added, "Mark of the man in those days, though, was how a fella handled Bill Denson." I knew who he meant. Bill Denson was a brilliant but erratic man, who had been disbarred for life for some of his antics in the courtroom. He could always be found in the Birmingham Law Library wearing the same outfit—cowboy hat, black patent leather boots with whipcord pants tucked into them, and a long-sleeved purple shirt. If you got close to him, you'd think he always wore the same purple shirt.

In my father's day, when Bill Denson was practicing law, he dressed the same, except that he always carried a .32 pistol, which he used to dominate the courtroom. One day Bill drew on Borden Burr right in Judge Smith's courtroom with the jury in the box. Borden, not a man to be intimidated by anyone, whipped out his .45 and it looked as if there were going to be a shoot-out when Judge Smith saved the day by crying out, "Gentlemen, gentlemen, think of these jurors and their families." He came down off the bench, disarmed them and confiscated their guns.

Judge Smith told me once, "The time Hugo had his run-in with Bill, Bill had broadcast around town how he was gonna show this damn Hugo Black who was boss in the courtroom. So I watched 'em good when they came in. This time Hugo was representing an insurance company —something rare for him. I'd go out in the hall on the recesses, because I was expecting trouble from Bill. Sure enough, it came. Hugo cut up one of Bill's witnesses bad on cross-examination. During that recess, I saw Bill walk up to Hugo in the hall. He pulled out his pistol and stuck it in Hugo's ribs and said, 'You sonofabitch. You're not fooling with some little old tiddledeewink now—you're fooling with Bill Denson. You smart-ass another of my witnesses, and I'll shoot your ass in its tracks.' Ole Hugo never moved a muscle. He just said: 'Bill, get away from here. You shoot me and I'll crawl off to the magistrate to get a warrant out against you for assault with intent to kill, no matter how true the shot. Now get out of here before I walk down for a plain assault warrant. Well, maybe that isn't necessary—Judge C. B.'s watching now.' Bill looked and saw me and put up the pistol. Hugo said Bill never bothered him again after that."

In those days, Hugo was something of a star. Because there were only a few movie houses, and no television or theatrical productions, the lawyers were the best show in town. His reputation always preceded him wherever he went, and whenever he was scheduled to try a case, the courthouse would draw a crowd.

Some of the techniques Daddy used to win cases involving black people were later in his career seized upon wrongfully to charge him as a racist. Although it would have pained him to admit it, he was not beyond exploiting an emotional feeling based on race if that helped his client. In one case he defended a Methodist preacher who had killed a Catholic priest for marrying the preacher's daughter to a Puerto Rican. In order to help his client get off on the basis of "temporary insanity" and self-defense, Hugo used every means he could—even, some people say, pulling the shades down in the courtroom to emphasize the dark skin of the Puerto Rican. Since Alabama juries were all-white in those days, it is not inconceivable that he may have used this tactic. If indeed this was the case, I believe that the record will show that Hugo offered sufficient evidence—based on such facts as where the principals were standing at the time of the shooting and the mechanics of the homicide—to prove that the murder was not premeditated. If pulling down the shades helped to prove this, he certainly owed it to his client under the advocate system to do this.

Another case involving race took place in a cotton-mill town in Alabama. I don't think the historians have discovered this one yet. The deputy sheriff, whom I shall call Lou James, had a younger brother who had been an overseer of a plantation when a dispute arose between himself and one of his black workers. The story goes that the black killed his overseer and was then tried for murder. Daddy never told me why, but the all-white jury acquitted the black man. Afterwards in a jubilant mood some black men lifted the man on their shoulders and carried him away from the courthouse. Lou was standing under a mulberry tree watching all this, when suddenly he pulled out his pistol and shot the black. He was killed.

Daddy defended Lou against a murder charge. Although he pleaded "not guilty" for his client, he later told me, "It was inexcusable, Son, but Lou was my friend, so I had to help him."

In his argument, he read from Rousseau's *Social Contract* and Sir Henry Maine's *Ancient Law,* in which he found that it was the duty of the oldest son—when the father had died—to avenge the killing of other members of the family. Finally, he told the jury: "When Lou saw his brother's killer on the shoulders of those fellas, he just sort of exploded—his mind blew apart. This noble fella blew to pieces. Who knows what went on out there between Lou's brother and the dead man. They are both dead. In a scrap, who knows who is right? Lou lost his control. For that he is to blame. As for me, family loyalty is a great thing. I understand what Lou did. He loved his brother and he just blew apart. What would be served by convicting him? Nothing! All of us know Lou will never harm another soul if he is—if he is [and here a tear rolled down Daddy's cheek]—if he is not thrown in with a lot of bad people."

Lou was acquitted.

Whenever Hugo represented a plaintiff, such as an injured miner, against a large corporation which was incorporated in another state, Daddy always brought suit in Alabama courts. His reason was simple: juries usually favor the poor over the rich, the individual over the corporation, the exploited over the exploiters, the weak over the strong, put it as you will. The judges of the state courts usually allowed the juries to determine the issues. The federal judges, on the other hand, were much more likely to direct a verdict against the plaintiff or to set aside a verdict for the plaintiff on the grounds that the case for the corporation was so clear that the jury could not rule for the plaintiff.

Because a foreign corporation could remove the case to the federal courts if the controversy involved $3,000 or more, Hugo would always sue for $2,999.99, except where an extraordinarily serious injury with perfectly documented facts was involved. "It was either accept this limit or nothing, Son, the way those federal judges behaved."

Once, however, he contrived an answer to the dilemma of limiting himself to $2,999.99. In his readings he discovered that in colonial America the judge had the right to instruct the jury on the law, but the jury had the absolute right after being instructed by the judge on the law to determine the case as it saw fit.

In his next case in federal court before Judge Billy Grubb, Daddy argued this proposition to the jury. Somehow it slipped by without objection or comment from Judge Grubb, but the jury did not miss it.

Judge Grubb instructed the jury routinely on the law of the case and told them it was the function of the jury to apply the law to the facts. But then Judge Grubb directed the jury to go out in the jury room and return a verdict for the defendant. Instead, they returned with a very substantial verdict for the plaintiff and stated that "the law as given to us by Your Honor required the verdict for the plaintiff, and, as Your Honor said, the jury applies the law to the facts—not the judge."

Judge Grubb asked the jury to retire and said to Daddy, "Hugo, either you tell that jury to obey my instructions to bring in a verdict for the defendant or I will hold you in contempt."

Daddy said, "Your Honor, I respect your office and I respect you as a man of the highest integrity, but I cannot, consistent with my duty, undertake to tell this jury what to do. That is your job. I have said nothing improper to this jury—the defendant did not object and neither did Your Honor."

"Very well, Mr. Black. Since you do not dispute my prerogative—Mr. Bailiff, dismiss the jury. Mr. Clerk, enter a verdict of not guilty for the defendant."

As a matter of form, the judge made an error; he had no right to order the entry of a false verdict nor to dismiss the jury. For some reason, my father did not appeal this decision, even though I am sure he originally intended to. Perhaps he had second thoughts about reestablishing this principle of colonial law because it could prove dangerous in times of minority persecutions. But then again, maybe he just figured he would lose.

Hugo's partnership with General H. Lee Randolph was doomed from the beginning because the life-styles of the two men were so different. The breakup came about mainly because of the General's habit of gambling regularly with professionals. Hugo did not believe in gambling because he thought it was foolish and likely to put you under the control of the wrong people.

Daddy told the General, "You can't win those fellas. They are professionals."

"Hugo," the General said, "I know the laws of mathematics. They do not know these laws. I am devising systems whereby it will be impossible for them to win and impossible for me to lose."

"Lee, did you ever think that they might be cheating on you? How is that variable going to fit in with your constants?"

"Hugo," the General said, "you worry about yourself, and I'll worry about myself."

"No, I can't do that, Lee. If you won't stop we'll just have to break up the partnership. I don't want those fellas to be able to get at me through you."

So that was the end of Black and Randolph.

Once when I was discussing with Daddy what his contemporaries at the bar had to say about him, he said, "Don't think I always won. I told you there are some things you just can't control." Then he told me about Mr. Ernest McFarland.

"Son, he always treated me so nice. He came to court in a patched-up suit representing the biggest corporations. He always smiled except when gravity was called for, and he never said anything bad about anybody. I would win but never very much, and Mac would always congratulate me. I remember my greatest cross-examination. Mac was on the other side. I had a hard case, and Mac had a witness who cut me to the bone on direct. I tell you, Son, I didn't know whether to cross-examine. But I decided the jury might feel I was afraid of him if I didn't. And right then, my client butted in and said, 'Take him on, Mr. Black. You can't let him get away with that stuff.' So, I eased in a question. It went pretty good. Then I tipped in a little bit farther. He bit at that one, and the next one went even better. When I got through, Son, my client told me that had to be the greatest cross-examination of all time. Out in the hall, the Judge and Mac both said the same thing. Funny thing, though, I didn't get enough money. I thought I ought to have ten thousand dollars, but I only got a couple of thousand."

"Daddy," I said, "I guess you just can't tell about trials. Must have been great, though, to bring off a cross-examination like that."

"Well, Son," he said, "the next morning when I walked into my office there was this fella I had torn up on cross-examination."

"What in the world did he want?"

"Well, he asked me for the fifty dollars my client had promised him if he testified like he did on cross-examination."

"Aw, Daddy, you're kidding."

"No. That's what he said. So all I could do was call Mac and tell him what had happened and tell him I would agree to a new trial. Now, that's the worst part. Mac just kind of cleared his throat and said, 'Hugo, I appreciate it, but I guess we can just let the verdict stand.' Rascal beat me even when my client paid off his best witness."

Campaigning for the U.S. Senate

Running for senator was a very ambitious undertaking for my father. Unlike most senatorial candidates in Alabama, he had held only one previous elective office, that of county solicitor, and so it was only natural that in the first days of his campaign, not many people considered him a serious contender. But Daddy had such extraordinary charisma that he was able to make thousands of Alabamians feel that he was their best friend. To this day when I meet an Alabamian new to my acquaintance, the first words I am likely to hear are "My grandfather was one of your father's best friends," or sometimes "I was one of your father's best friends." When I would report this back to my father, he might well say, "Fella is right. I remember his daddy, used to be school superintendent down in Baldwin County." Or if he could not remember right off, he would open his safe and pull out one of his black books, flip through it, and say, "He's right. His daddy put out my literature for me up in Etowah County."

From the very beginning, Hugo's political career was

built strictly upon personal contacts and platform magnetism. "I had to, Son. I didn't want and probably couldn't get big contributions. If I got them, they'd want something they shouldn't have and, besides that, most of them just plain didn't want me in office."

"Do you blame them?"

"Not those kind of fellas. No!"

Hugo felt that he had good backing in Jefferson County because of his having been county solicitor, his reputation as an attorney, and his years teaching Sunday School and attending lodge meetings. What he had to do now was make himself known throughout the state. A year before the election he began driving his Ford into counties he had never been in. At each seat he would get out and start to mosey around, stopping everybody to shake hands and introduce himself. "I'm Hugo Black, I'm glad to meet you. Who do you think around here could give me the most help in my campaign?" He would get a name. Then he might see a checkers game, walk up and introduce himself and watch. He knew that most rural Alabamians thought that excellence in checkers signified excellence of mind and character. After a while, he would say, "You know, I believe I can whip either of you fellas."

Then he would take on one and win, and laughingly say, "Who's the best checkers player around here?"

They would tell him.

"Go get him. Tell him, Senator Black challenges him."

No matter whether Hugo won or not, he would say, "Man, I need the help of a fella can play checkers like you. Let me send you some of my literature."

He always looked in a county for those leaders who possessed little wealth and could not be classified as "courthouse people"—the ones who seemed to be loved and respected by the most people in the county. During this initial campaigning, he made no speeches. He just drove and walked around, played checkers, shook hands and talked. Usually, some new friend would invite him to spend the night at his home, and he would stay right there with the whole family. Nobody went with him on those trips except occasionally a friend who had moved to Birmingham from the particular county he was visiting, and who would introduce Hugo around.

Whenever he returned to Birmingham, he would ship literature to his newly appointed managers in the counties and get them to set up a speaking engagement at a time when the people could be expected to be in town and in a good frame of mind. Then he started his speaking campaign, traveling anywhere he could get a hearing—in courtrooms, barns, churches; outdoors from courthouse steps, tree stumps, horse wagons, or pickup truck beds.

Hugo's tireless campaigning was still regarded by his opponents as a joke. Favored to win was John Bankhead, whose father had served in the Senate for over thirty years. Breck Musgrove, another opponent, was probably the richest man in Alabama by virtue of his coal mine interests, and the other candidate, Tom Kilby, had been governor and owned Kilby Steel in Anniston. But Hugo never relaxed his hard-driving campaign as the candidate of the plain people, and as Election Day neared, to almost everyone's surprise, it became apparent that Hugo Black was in the lead, and any doubts that his courtroom magic could carry over to the platform were now dispelled.

Unable to ignore him any longer, all the opponents began to attack his position any way they could. "This so-called man of the people," they said, "keeps a *Graham Paige* at home and drives his Model T Ford all over the state. This man is the richest lawyer in the state. The rich people are backing him."

But this simply was not so. The establishment hated and feared him, although it has been said that the establishment lawyers in Birmingham supported him because they wanted to get him out of their hair. He spent only $10,000 on the campaign, staying within the legal limit, and it was all his own money. He did not use the radio and advertised in the paper very little. He claimed that, in contrast, each of his opponents spent well in excess of $100,000, using some of their funds to pay family leaders to get a family vote, or paying off anyone who claimed a following. What really hurt Hugo, though, were some of the newspapermen. He had solid evidence that one prominent columnist took money on the sly to support another candidate. Perhaps his biggest disappointment came from the union leaders. He had represented unions when no one with comparable ability would, and he had always believed in the good they could do for workers. To see the local leaders' endorsements go to an opponent who despised the unions was very upsetting indeed.

Sometimes he would take my brother Sterling and me with him to campaign. He always introduced us and made sure that everyone knew he was a good family man. Most of the time, he would be assured of a new acquaintance's support. But sometimes, a man would say: "I'm sorry, but Bankhead is my friend."

Hugo would reply, "You should vote for him by all means. But I hope you will remember me some time when he isn't running against me."

If a man replied more harshly, saying, "I will not vote for you, sir. I don't agree with anything you stand for," then Hugo, unflustered, would say, "Well, I'm sorry. But I certainly appreciate your frankness."

This incredible effort on his part paid off, and Hugo won enough votes in the Democratic primary to automatically win the election. Although his biographers will labor over whether his Ku Klux Klan support or prohibition or whatever issue elected him, I don't believe any of this is really that important. He won because all of his opponents combined had not established one half the "best friendships" he enjoyed all over the state; because as a public speaker he radiated a natural, simple charm equal to that of any great politician or trial lawyer; and because people believed he would work for their interest instead of his own or that of a few privileged friends.

The
Fosters

~❧

My mother's parents, the Fosters, were an integral part of
our family life in those days. My grandfather, Dr. Sterling
J. Foster, was a character I found entertaining, but he was
a terrible burden to Mama and to Daddy.

By the time I came along, he had pretty well dropped
out of the rat race. In his early sixties he was still slender
and sported an impressive white mustache. Most of the
time he was nattily dressed in Daddy's castoff clothes,
which for some reason looked better on him than on my
father. His voice was rich and deep, making him a perfect
bass in any choir. He also read a great deal and remembered much of what he read, which appealed to Daddy.
But he was slow getting anything done, and this drove his
son-in-law crazy.

Dr. Foster was an old-time Southern gentleman, born
just as the War Between the States ended. Grandaddy's
father, a doctor, owned much of Bullock County in Alabama, and few of his slaves left when they were given
their freedom. From the time he was a child, Sterling had

a young black boy waiting on him and even dressing him until he was thirty years old; he even went to college with Sterling and then accompanied him to Europe, where Sterling studied in Germany and Scotland. Sterling made a book of pen-and-ink sketches while he was in Europe, which I saw later and thought remarkably fine. Unfortunately, although he had great artistic talent, he had given up drawing by the time I knew him.

Returning to Memphis, Sterling met and married Ann Patterson, whose father was a congressman and the largest donor to the parish fund. They moved to Birmingham, and Granddaddy took over the South Highlands Presbyterian Church. Sterling's father's death brought the young couple a half-million-dollar inheritance, and with the births of Sterling Foster, Jr., Josephine and Virginia, the family became well established in the town.

Trouble was in store for them, however. It had been brewing in the church over Dr. Foster's sermons. Some very influential members of the congregation didn't think Granddaddy was literal enough in his interpretation of the Bible, and they were annoyed when he suggested that Jonah might not have really been swallowed by the whale. Finally, Dr. Foster was told that he could either teach the Bible their way or leave the church. After much agonizing, Dr. Foster made a very courageous decision. He defied them and was fired. All this caused my grandfather considerable emotional upheaval, and he suffered what you might call a nervous breakdown.

When he got himself together again, he tried selling insurance for a while. He had enough contacts whom he would visit, but unless they asked him to sell them a policy, he would not degrade himself by asking them to buy. And whenever he invested in an insurance or real estate agency, he always lost money. By the time my father married Josephine, Granddaddy had blown $500,000 and had no income.

Hugo offered help, but Granddaddy was too much of a proud Southern gentleman to accept any. But my grandmother reported that Sterling was bankrupt and was literally hiding his bills under the rug. To avoid hurting my grandparents' feelings, Daddy figured out how much it would take to enable them to live reasonably well, and then offered to move into their house at a rental figure equal to what they would need to live, plus a little extra to take care of their habits of luxury. They agreed—after all, any honorable man could take on boarders—and the Black family moved into the elegant gabled brownstone house at 1313 Niazuma Avenue.

Because Dr. Foster insisted, I slept in the same room with him, and as a result I never got enough sleep. He would come home around lunchtime, take a "little medicine" (100 proof) and then drop into bed for his nap, which lasted a good three hours. Since he had slept so long in the afternoon, he always woke up around four in the morning and switched on his lamp. Lighting up a cigarette, he would say in his rich, melodious bass, "Bud, are you awake?"

If I hadn't been, I was. Then he would bring up something he had been reading about, or read aloud a passage from Macaulay or Bobby Burns (but never the Bible). In contrast to Daddy, who tended to understate, Dr. Foster always overstated everything. Both were alike in their enthusiasm for language, but Daddy would always praise a book sparingly, while Grandaddy, on the other hand, felt that everything he read was "the greatest thing ever written." In his defense, though, I should point out that his great love of books kept his mind active and alert up until he died, and he enjoyed nothing better than learning something new about history or politics or language.

Granddaddy was a man of many prejudices. According to his "missing link" theory, the black man proved Darwin's theory of evolution, since he was the "link" between the ape and the white man. Granted, Granddaddy was always courteous and affectionate with the blacks he came into contact with, but he expected them "to stay in their place." He, like everybody in the Black family except Daddy and Mama, would chastise me if I referred to a black man as a "gentleman" or a black woman as a "lady," which I frequently did just by instinct and out of respect. Once, after my father was on the Supreme Court, Granddaddy exploded at Daddy and me about our egalitarian attitude toward blacks and warned that our views would produce a "jungle," that he himself would not be hurt because of the little time he had left, but that it would do us in.

He had each nationality tagged, and he could hate with a magnificent passion. All restaurants were operated by Greeks, except Chinese restaurants, he told me, and he believed that Jews were responsible for all scheming, deception and fraud in business that could not be attributed to Lebanese, Italians, or his particular alien hate of the day.

The symbol of the depth of his hatred was what he did to "get" the Japs in the Second World War. We had a magnificent rose garden, but periodically it would be invaded by Japanese beetles, which chewed up a good part of it. Granddaddy was convinced that nothing like that had ever occurred before the war and that Hirohito had dispatched this horde of beetles as a part of his war effort. "These Japs are low enough to crawl under a snake's belly with a top hat on," he would exclaim, or, "These Japs are low-browed hounds." One day after imbibing his Old Fashioneds he declared he had had his fill of Hirohito's conniving, and mustering all the cigarette lighters in the house, he proceeded to the rose garden, where he commenced to burn out the Japanese beetles from the rose blooms. He gave old Hirohito what he had coming until the lighter fluid gave out.

A concomitant of Granddaddy's capacity to hate was his capacity for loyalty. He used to hate John L. Lewis, the head of the United Mine Workers, and frequently labeled him a "criminal," "communist," and "traitor." But after I started to represent Lewis, Granddaddy regarded him as a "labor statesman," even when he "struck against the government." Although Granddaddy reserved the right to disagree with Daddy, he would not tolerate this in anyone else. If anyone criticized Hugo too strongly, Dr. Foster would indignantly end the conversation with "What would you expect of a man who stands around with his jaws hanging open." Or, "What could you expect of a nitwit." How he avoided getting slugged I will never know.

The Doctor was a real problem to Daddy. He longed to be important and to have achieved as much as his son-in-law. To make his mark, he needed help from Hugo. Yet he could not bring himself to ask directly for anything. So he went about it by indirection.

When a postmaster's job came up, Hugo had his man

in mind—Cooper Green—but he heard disquieting rumors that there was another candidate, Dr. Sterling Foster, even though the candidate had never approached him. Instead, hearing Cooper was Hugo's favorite, Dr. Foster approached Cooper and solicited his support. Cooper, figuring he could not win in a contest with the father-in-law of the man who would make the appointment, agreed to help Dr. Foster, and paid a call on Hugo. When Cooper got there and made his pitch for Dr. Foster, Daddy winced. The Doctor had him cornered. So Daddy thanked Cooper and sent him on his way.

But Hugo was not finished. He went to his library, and found that you had to be under sixty-five years of age to qualify for the appointment. Daddy then asked Cooper over and instructed him to inform the candidate, Dr. Foster, that the law required a postmaster to be under sixty-five.

Cooper departed. Within a day he returned. "The Doctor said he was glad to have that news," he told Daddy, "but he failed to understand what relevance that had to him because he has a while to go yet before he is sixty-five."

Daddy, of course, knew the Doctor was sixty-seven; Mama had just recently thrown a birthday party for him. Daddy went back to the library and made some calls. He then summoned Cooper back.

"Cooper," he said, "will you tell the candidate that the oath of office calls for a deposition under oath that you are under sixty-five and that the code of the United States provides up to ten years for a false affidavit of age for the job as postmaster?"

The next time Cooper reported back, he said, "Senator,

the candidate has asked me to tell you that he does not understand the reference—it has no relevance to his situation—but he has withdrawn, and you are free to appoint anybody you wish."

The next day Hugo appointed Cooper.

The indirect means of support Daddy had to provide the Doctor were many. Granddaddy would go to the bank and borrow on the strength of being Daddy's father-in-law. He, of course, could not pay back the loan. When Granddaddy could not come up with the money on the due date, Hugo would have to pay. I never realized the circuitousness necessary for Daddy to support Granddaddy until one day Daddy called me up to the study and asked me to do a favor for him. He gave me a letter addressed to Granddaddy at the house and asked me to take it to the corner and mail it. I said, "I'll just take it downstairs and give it to him. Why go through all this trouble?"

"No, Son. He won't take it. Do as I say," and I did.

I should make it clear that the Doctor never borrowed any money for his own personal pleasure. He always used the borrowed money to pay off debts incurred in ventures where he had been exploited by unscrupulous businessmen. Granddaddy was a favorite mark for promoters because he trusted people wholeheartedly, and brilliant as he was, he could never quite believe that a businessman would purposely try to take advantage of him. The only person he really ever deceived was himself.

Unfortunately, the Doctor used his status as Hugo Black's father-in-law to throw his weight around more than he should have. Once, when we were driving back to Birmingham from Washington with a couple of friends of mine, we were stopped by a policeman because I had been speeding. The policeman was courteous and said he would have to give me a ticket, since I was going eighty-five in a fifty-five zone. But then Grandaddy leaned over and said, "Do you know who this boy is?"

"Yes," said the policeman. "He is Hugo Black, Jr."

"Don't you know that his father is Supreme Court Justice Black? Why, he will have your job for this! What is the matter with you!"

"Officer," I said, "don't pay any attention to my granddaddy. You do to me what your duty requires. My daddy would not have you do anything else."

"Now wait a minute, Bud."

"Hush, Granddaddy," I said. "Daddy will fuss at me for speeding like this, but that's all right."

"Bud."

"Hush," I said. "I'm sorry, Officer."

"Go on, son, and tell your granddaddy he almost got you put in jail."

Granddaddy's visits to Washington always produced a crisis. Mama would go to pieces. Daddy said it was because he burdened Mama, and he did. He would pour out all his frustrations, telling her how he had been plagued by bad luck financially and how he would make it up to her with a big strike, in insurance, graphite—first one thing, then another. Although Hugo strongly objected to his presence when he saw how it upset Josephine, there were times when the Doctor could amuse Hugo with one of his little jokes.

We were at dinner one evening when Daddy and I began kidding the Doctor about the fact that he never helped with the dishes. In reply, Granddaddy grabbed hold of the rim of a glass with his thumb and index finger, and holding it away from his body as if it were some execrable insect, he took it into the kitchen while solemnly intoning, "Never let it be said that Dr. Sterling J. Foster never carried in any dishes."

The Doctor's good humor did temper the annoyance he caused when visiting, as this letter Daddy wrote me indicates:

"Your granddaddy is in this section, although he left for New York this morning. At the present moment, as I understand it, he is about to become fabulously wealthy, through the sale of certain mineral lands in Clay County, Alabama. He has already planned a most lavish distribution. Probably your past experience has caused you to realize your granddaddy's inability to act on the old maxim that a bird in the hand is worth two in the bush. At any rate, he continues in good health, enjoys life about as much as any man I ever knew, and has an unlimited capacity to digest an extraordinary amount of food."

Although Granddaddy was invariably courteous to people of different races he was prejudiced against, he sometimes displayed his likes and dislikes in the most embarrassing scenes. On one occasion he went to a party with us at the Thurman Arnolds'. This great, lovable, kooky genius of a law professor was also a man of vast enthusiasms about his current projects. He had once been a U.S. Court of Appeals judge in the District of Columbia, but had served only a couple of years and retired "because he could not make enough money." I don't believe, though, that this was the real reason; he had retired because he was bored and had no impartiality in him. Thurman Arnold was partial down to his bone marrow. This particular party was at a time when Senator Joe McCarthy was running wild, and Thurman Arnold, Abe Fortas and their firm were defending, free of charge, government employees caught in McCarthy's net. It was a truly noble endeavor—some say the last truly noble endeavor of "the Washington lawyers." In any event, Judge Arnold, at the head of the table, opined with typical gusto, "This loyalty thing is a goddamned outrage."

Granddaddy quickly agreed with him.

"It's a damnable outrage," said Judge Arnold. "Why, the people they are trying to purge deserve a medal, not censure."

Granddaddy dropped his fork, coughed up his food into his napkin and said, "Sir, they don't deserve a damned medal at all. They don't deserve a trial. They should be dragged out by their heels and strung up by the neck to the nearest tree."

Judge Arnold dropped his utensils onto his plate and looked Granddaddy in the eye and said, "Doctor, that is fascist talk."

Granddaddy fired back, "Sir, you are a communist." At that point Mama fled the table to Judge Arnold's study and began to weep. The Doctor and Judge Arnold left the room in a huff.

It was an unfortunate incident, especially since Judge Arnold was representing Granddaddy and his friends with the graphite company in a questionable case as a favor to Mama, and I'm sure Judge Arnold really got a great charge out of Granddaddy. I turned to my father and said, "You get Judge Arnold, I'll get Granddaddy. We'll bring them together and then bring them in to Mama."

When I found the Doctor, I told him, "You ought to be

ashamed to hurt Mama like that." He hung his head. "C'mon now, let's go talk with the Judge and resume where we were when this foolishness started."

Daddy had done his job well. Both acted as if nothing had happened, the party continued, and we all had a splendid time.

Whenever we were on the road from Birmingham to Washington, we were treated to other examples of the Doctor's violent talk. As we passed through East Tennessee, his bristles would be up, since he regarded this as enemy territory because the people here had fought on the Union side. The Doctor complained if we stopped for directions; according to him, they were all nitwits and would not know the way. He often pointed out battle sites to me, saying something like "See that hill, Bud, we cut their guts out there, drove 'em right back off of it with knives, didn't have any ammunition, but that didn't stop our boys." When we finally arrived in Washington, we were not permitted to use the Memorial Bridge when he was in the car because we would have to go past the Lincoln Memorial.

Granddaddy's attitude toward the Civil War contrasted strongly with my father's. Hugo would have been on the side of the Union during the war, not only because he hated the thought of any war except the one with Hitler, but also because he despised slavery. He felt that "hotheads" had driven the South into the hopeless conflict with the North in order to keep their property, the slaves, and to further their own self-aggrandizement. Hugo's pet Civil War culprit was William Yancey, whom he thought blessed with extraordinary gifts, but who failed to use them in the public interest. Daddy admired the "free State of Winston," a county in northwest Alabama, which had remained loyal to the Union during the war. The Doctor, on the other hand, professed to believe that every man, woman and child in that county should have been executed by firing squad, hanging, or as he once said, "by the most torturous means conceived by man or God."

My father was also bothered by Granddaddy's attitude toward Nana. Although the Doctor always treated his wife respectfully and professed the greatest fondness for her, he never displayed any tenderness and he nearly always stayed some distance from her. So far as I could see, they could as well have been divorced during the time I knew them—a most civilized, respectful divorce, but a divorce nevertheless.

Granddaddy got a lot of satisfaction out of living as long as he did. He used to read the obituaries as friend after friend died, always professing great sadness, but you could see that he really felt pride in outliving each old friend who preceded him to the universal kingdom. His time started to come when they discovered a skip in his heartbeat and put him on digitalis. Not long after that, we learned from his landlady that he was not able to fend for himself in the apartment he had moved into from Niazuma Avenue after Nana died. I, of course, could not have him live with me because I knew he would destroy my home with his ways. My father and I agreed that the best place for him would be a nice retirement home.

After a search for a suitable place, we finally chose the Methodist home in Charlotte, North Carolina. The Doctor had a lovely room there and many recreational and medical facilities, everything a lively-minded oldster needed, except for one thing—they did not allow "medicine." We remedied that by smuggling his "medicine" in to him in his Hadocol bottle. For a while, he really did nicely. He conducted church services, gave Sunday School lessons, read constantly and even began to learn Spanish. But then he got glaucoma and could not read, and from then on he deteriorated rapidly.

Granddaddy died a few months later. I was there to ship his body off to Washington to be buried next to Nana.

Senator Hugo L. Black
of Alabama

੭ੳ

The official part of Daddy's Senate career is not really a very important part of my story. In those days, my brother Sterling and I cared little for what went on in the Senate. We would only want to go to the office with Daddy if he let us ride the subway train that runs from the Capitol to the Senate Office Building. Once, he invited us to go down to hear the President address Congress. We declined, preferring to play. Daddy shook his head in disgust and said, "When I was ten years old I would have given anything to get to hear the President speak."

However, he did get the whole family over to the Capitol one evening for a night session, an evening I'll never forget. Huey Long was filibustering, and Joe Robinson, the Democratic floor leader from Arkansas, had asked Hugo to try to stop him. The Kingfish considered Hugo to be a people's advocate like himself, and chances were that he would yield the floor to Hugo when he would not to anyone else for fear the opposition might try to take the floor away even though honor-bound to give it back as a matter of unwritten Senate law.

As we seated ourselves in the gallery, Mother explained to Sterling and me that Daddy would try to find out how long Huey planned to continue, and then, if that would disrupt the business of the Senate too much, he would try to find out what compromise might be acceptable to Huey on the matter that had set him off. Then as we peered over the railing we saw Hugo stand up as the Kingfish read a recipe for creole gumbo. I do not remember the exact words, but the substance went like this:

"Senator," Daddy said, "would the Senator yield for a question?"

"I will yield for a question from the Senator from Alabama," Huey replied.

"Senator," said Daddy, "how long does it take that stuff to cook?"

"This recipe," said Huey, "takes as many days, weeks, months and years, sir, as it has the energy to bubble."

"Isn't there some stuff, Senator, you can throw into it to make the gumbo edible in an hour or two, like some special kind of shrimp or something like that?"

"Sir," said Huey, "shrimp do not have what it takes to speed the cooking time. It takes whale meat to change the cooking time."

"Surely not the whole whale, Senator."

"No, Senator, just the choice part."

"Thank you, Senator. That answers my question."

Hugo walked over to Joe Robinson, and they conferred for a while. The filibuster ended shortly afterward when Senator Long yielded for Daddy's next question, from which Senator Long deduced that the choice part of the whale was available.

I do not know exactly what kind of a United States senator my father was in his first or second term. But I do know that he was as dissatisfied with his first term as he was satisfied with his second term. Both my mother and father told me about the talk they had right after Daddy was reelected to his second term in 1932.

Hugo had a sixth sense about what the voters in Alabama wanted at any particular time. There was no need for him to take any poll, he just knew. "Darling," he said to Josephine, "I've been following too much what it seems like to me the voters in Alabama want. I can keep on doing that and I can stay on in the job the rest of my life. But I don't think that's what a great United States senator ought to do."

"What is he supposed to do?" Mama asked.

"Well, he is supposed to act for the national interest when it conflicts with his state's interest. He ought to do everything he can for his state's interest when it's consistent with the national interest, but the national interest should be first. It's also his job to lead the voters in his state, not to follow them. If he can't convince them he's right, they can throw him out. I don't want to be one of these wind-testers who pander to the worst in the people."

"Honey," my mother replied, "that's risky and maybe presumptuous too."

"Yeah, it is," Daddy said, "but George Norris runs the risk and he's the greatest senator of all. That is what I've *got* to do. If you're willing, I'm ready to run the risk."

"Of course I am," Mama answered.

"I'm glad," he said. "I feel like a new man."

Actually, Daddy had started growing as a senator soon after his election to a first term. In those days the salary of a United States senator was only $10,000 a year, with few of the extras both senators and congressmen enjoy today. Hugo saw nothing wrong with continuing his practice as long as he didn't represent clients who had any interest in matters pending before the Senate. But he soon learned differently. He used to tell this story on himself, his eyes twinkling: "I had known for some time that I was the greatest man in final argument in the state and the greatest cross-examiner around, but, after I became senator, I noticed an astounding change. My jury verdicts for plaintiffs jumped clear out of sight. I won an impossible criminal case. I thought maybe I had hit another one of those plateaus these psychologists talk about. Then it hit me. 'I wonder if any of these jurors will feel I'm obligated to 'em and want favors from me?' I said to myself. Well, I didn't have too long to wait. There may be a few who did not call on me later, but I can't remember who they were. So I had to give up the practice."

After this, he felt strongly about senators and congressmen who continued to practice law after their election. "They're worse than I was, Son. They don't even practice any law. They just put their names on the door and take money. Why, a fella who sat next to me in the Senate got a hundred thousand dollars a year from a steel company. And then some of these senator-lawyers put their partners on the federal bench. Really builds up the firm's federal practice. It's trouble. How're the people gonna have any confidence in fellas who do that? A man who serves in a public office has no business at all making money out of the office. But some of them have ten thousand bad reasons why they ought to be able to." If Hugo had stayed on in the Senate, I am sure that he would have pushed a stringent law prohibiting senators and congressmen from profiting from outside ventures.

Although it has been said that he was a loner in the Senate, from the indications he gave me it seems that he became an accepted member of the "club" early in his Senate career. As always, he maintained a certain reserve and independence; yet from the start he got good committee assignments, and many treated him with a warmth and respect usually reserved for the senior senators. Some of this early acceptance came because of recognition of his own abilities. But much of it was undoubtedly the result of my mother's influence. Without ever trying, Mama had always ended up as president of whatever ladies' club she happened to be in. It turned out that the Senate Ladies Luncheon Club was no exception. She very quickly became very popular with the senators' wives. One who became especially interested in her was Mrs. Walter George, wife of Senator George of Georgia, a very powerful member of the "club," and a man who was reputed to be *the* voice on foreign affairs. Senator George got much of his financial support from the Georgia Power Company and, of course, viewed public affairs quite differently than Hugo did, but such was my mother's influence on Mrs. George that her husband eventually became something of a sponsor for Daddy. Mrs. Hiram Johnson also loved Mama, and as a result Republican Senator Johnson of California showed interest in Hugo. The red-headed Senator Jim "Ham" Lewis of Illinois and William Gibbs

McAdoo of California were smitten by Mama, and, as Daddy said, "They treat me nice to be around your mother."

Those leaders with liberal views took to my father right from the start. Probably the senator most respected by his colleagues while Daddy served in the Senate was George Norris of Nebraska. Senator Norris always voted his conscience without regard to what it would do to him at the polls. He also had the moral courage to stand alone against the world when he thought this was the right thing to do —for example, he had risked a great deal by voting against the entry of the United States into the First World War. "Quite often," my father once told me, "you will find a fella like Senator Norris has got a watermelon-sized ego and is insufferable. Or he's like they used to say about John Lilburne: 'If the world was emptied of all but John Lilburne, Lilburne would quarrel with John and John would quarrel with Lilburne.' But George Norris isn't that way at all. He is gentle and unassuming, but firm and immovable in his conviction when he knows he is right." George Norris is the only contemporary of my father's who could be classified as one of his heroes. I have always had the feeling that except for Norris, Daddy felt he was as good as or better than any other contemporary.

Hugo possessed the same rugged independence as Senator Norris. Not only did he have it and prize it, but it characterized those members of his family he most admired. His older sister, Ora, is a case in point. Ora, who for many years taught school in Clay County, worshiped Hugo and would listen to no talk comparing her other brothers' abilities to Hugo's. "There was something special and extra about Hugo from the start," she would say.

"It was almost as if he had been sent from another world." Although Ora married twice and raised children by each marriage, there came a time when she was alone in the world. Daddy felt that he owed her much of the credit for whatever success he had achieved, and he wanted very much to support her. But she had never taken a dime from him, and she would not then. Neither would she live with or accept a dime from her children. Instead she went to work in a garment factory in Connecticut, and when she could no longer continue this, she sewed at home, supporting herself in this manner until her death.

It's not surprising then that what troubled Hugo most about his second term in the Senate was the label "rubber stamp" that the newspapers hung on him. They claimed that whatever President Roosevelt proposed, Daddy "rubber-stamped"; the President commanded and Senator Black responded like a tin soldier.

This simply was not true. President Roosevelt let it be known to Congress that the National Industrial Recovery Act (N.I.R.A.) represented the very heart of his program for dealing with the depression. Hugo felt that the bill simply proposed to suspend the anti-trust laws and let businessmen get together and fix prices. Not only did Hugo object to violating the Sherman Anti-Trust Act, he also did not agree with the bill's premise that ruinous competition among businessmen had caused the depression.

My father was convinced that the depression resulted from too little purchasing power of the needy consumer, and that this in turn resulted from too little return for the worker for his labor and too large a return for capital or those managing it. According to him, "The N.R.A. is a price-fixer's dream. It will only aggravate the trouble. These businessmen will just jack prices up and put goods further out of reach of the people who really need them and further line the pockets of those who have more than enough."

Despite pressure from the White House and organized labor, which supported the bill because of a collective bargaining provision, as well as some of his closest friends in Congress, Hugo fought the N.R.A. with all his resources. He lost—except in one respect. He predicted that the Supreme Court would declare the N.R.A. unconstitutional, and his prediction came true.

Although FDR was well aware of Hugo's opposition to the N.R.A., there did come a time when the President tried to influence Daddy by threats. Senator Pat McCarran of Nebraska had offered an amendment to President Roosevelt's bill to create the Public Works Administration. The President proposed that the wages for public work should be $50 a month. The McCarran amendment would require the government to pay no set figure but, instead, the "prevailing wage" in the area where the work would take place. Hugo indicated his support for the McCarran amendment, whereupon he immediately received a telephone call from the President. When the President could not sweet-talk him into changing his position, his tone turned bitter.

"Hugo," he said, "if you and your group do not change your vote, I am going to have to discipline you. I will have to go on the radio against you."

"Mr. President," Daddy said, "I would not use that type of tactic if I were you. I intend to vote my conviction on the McCarran amendment. It is my conscientious feeling that it, rather than your proposal, is the bill that is in the public interest. I am sure that a man of your mettle and stripe would never alter his course of action because of a threat of any kind and that you would have no respect for a friend like me—and I am your friend—if I altered mine. Mr. President, you have been working too hard, and when anyone, even a President, works too hard he sometimes does things that do not reflect his own personality."

The President then changed the subject and initiated a pleasant conversation. My father, of course, voted for the McCarran amendment.

Daddy always felt that a congressman, or any public servant, should be able to give and take criticism. Even though he himself got angry many times when he was criticized, he told me he knew it was wrong: "The worst thing you can do is get puffed up with self-importance." I think that is why he always had a pet peeve about chauffeured limousines. "First thing every one of these nuts wants when he gets to Washington is a chauffeured limousine." As far as he was concerned, neither congressmen nor, for that matter, corporation executives needed such a thing. They could use a car pool.

Hugo soon became known as the Senate's toughest and most skillful investigator. In 1933, when the Democrats in Congress became suspicious of the ocean mail subsidy program in which shipping companies received substantial subsidies to ensure an adequate U.S. merchant marine fleet of ships, Hugo headed a committee to investigate the matter. Shortly afterward, he also looked into airmail contracts. Then in 1935, when the public utilities holding company bill came before Congress, Hugo headed a committee to check into the lobbying activities.

In all of these investigations, Hugo's committees turned up grossly improper activities by people in the highest places. He showed that management frequently siphoned off the subsidies through subcontracts with dummy corporations controlled by management, with phantom wages and salaries, phony purchases and other patently crooked devices and schemes. It came to light also that management was paying itself exorbitant salaries and luxury expenses out of these government subsidies. Moreover, he proved that the amounts of the subsidies often were computed on the basis of false cost reports submitted by the companies. He even uncovered the fact that the overwhelming mail senators and congressmen received against the public utility holding company bill was, in the main, fraudulent; that most of the names on the letters they received had been taken from headstones in graveyards.

As a result of these investigations, a close watch was kept on the transfer of government subsidies to shipping and airline companies. And important legislation regulating the activities of lobbyists was passed. But Hugo also felt that there should be a continuing investigation into *all* transactions in which money flowed from the government or from the public to private corporations or companies. "And it ought to be conducted in such a way that the investigating personnel changes periodically by lot or some other chance method. Otherwise, they will get to the investigators."

Hugo suffered much criticism in his relentless pursuit of evidence. Few people realized, however, that he made personal sacrifices to stick to his beliefs. There was the case of a lawyer who was the husband of Mama's best friend in Washington. This man had been given critical documents by his clients in the hope that Hugo—in deference to Mama—would not embarrass the lawyer even if he did not give up the documents. But they did not know Hugo; he insisted on having the documents. The lawyer, claiming the lawyer-client privilege, refused, but Hugo persisted. The client then allegedly broke into the lawyer's office and destroyed the documents. "You promised to preserve those documents," Hugo told the lawyer, and then he caused contempt of the Senate proceedings to be brought against the lawyer, who was convicted and sentenced to a ten-day jail term.

After the hearings, Hugo was definitely prejudiced against special interest lobbyists, Washington lawyers and "legislative specialists." If they were up to any good, they would have a difficult time proving it to him. He also assumed thereafter that somewhere along the line, fraud was involved whenever money went from the government to private industry in the form of subsidies or contracts or whenever money came into corporations from the public in a stock or bond sale. And he developed a theory that he thought he could prove if he had the opportunity: "Except for windfall land profits, most great fortunes can be traced back to transactions with the government or the public in a stock or bond sale."

Sometimes he didn't even have to look very hard to discover a gross misuse of public funds. "At least the kind of stuff I discovered during my investigations involved attempts to conceal. I caught one the other day where they were so bold they didn't even bother to conceal what they were doing. This Alabama congressman and a group own Dauphin Island down in Mobile Bay. If I hadn't caught them, the government was going to build them a bridge out to Dauphin Island which overnight would have made their worthless land infinitely valuable. So you really can't exclude windfall profits on land from my theory that great fortunes track back to the government's treasury."

Of all his accomplishments in the Senate, he was proudest of what he had been able to do for people who worked with their hands. When in 1941 I was working for the U. S. Forest Service at the Kaniksu National Forest in Sandpoint, Idaho, protecting white pine trees from blister rust by pulling up wild gooseberry bushes, he once wrote to me: "All physical labor, followed day in and day out, is a tax and a burden. You can now better understand, I imagine, why I have devoted so much of my own time and energies to enactment of laws designed to shorten the working hours, alleviate working conditions, improve wages, and grant a greater increase of security to those who work at hard labor—not merely a short time in the summer—but all through the year. And what you make now, or even less, is the monthly pay of millions, not just for the worker, but his family as large or larger than ours. And it is true that many work in surroundings which do not improve but detract from their opportunity to have healthy bodies."

As if it were his own personal problem, Hugo worried about what would happen to the family of a workingman if he either lost his job unexpectedly, became sick, suffered an accident or died. For years, Hugo battled for passage of the Black-Connery bill, which would abolish child labor, set a minimum wage and shorten work hours. Some of his most vociferous opponents were Southerners who were afraid industry would no longer be lured to the South by cheap labor. Finally, a modified version of the bill was approved by the Senate; although it never did pass the House, it did form the basis of the Fair Labor Standards Act of 1938. If Hugo wasn't able to accomplish everything he would have liked to do for the working-man, he was able to at least help in providing the legislative foundation for a more decent life.

The Senator's Son

When I was seven years old and in the first grade at Oyster School behind the Wardman Park Hotel, where we lived in Washington, I came down with pneumonia. At first, Daddy fussed at me. "Son," he said, "you just won't wear your leggings and rubbers in this snow. I told you a hundred times the weak spot in the Blacks is the respiratory system—now maybe you'll listen." It made me mad and redoubled my determination never to wear leggings and rubbers. But I got worse, and fluid filled both lungs. Our doctor, Dr. Foot, told the family that I now had double pneumonia.

This was in the days before antibiotics. Mama stayed in the room with me practically every minute of the day. She kept ice packs on me, took my temperature, read me stories, and even slept right in the same bed with me. Frequently during the day Daddy would call from the floor of the Senate to find out how I was doing.

One afternoon I heard Dr. Foot say, "Josephine, you've got to reconcile yourself. Little Hugo may die."

That hit me hard. I recalled the first time I ever realized just what dying meant. I was about three years old, walking across the living room, singing, when in a flash the meaning of dying pervaded every muscle and bone of my body. I fell to the floor and cried softly to myself, "Oh, God, God, one day I just won't be anymore." But this time, after the initial shock, I gradually relaxed and re-signed myself to the possibility. But it was too much for Mama. She came down with pneumonia too.

This was when Daddy came into the picture. He moved a cot into my room, sent away the nurses and took over everything. Every minute I was slated for the graveyard, Daddy was there fighting. He never left my side. Once I heard Dr. Foot say to Daddy, "Nobody can live with that temperature, Hugo."

"Don't say that, Foot." Daddy replied. "It's just not true. Hugo can and he will."

It was then that I started feeling like fighting too. With Daddy holding an ice pack and keeping his finger on my pulse almost constantly, I knew I would make it because he believed I would.

Even then, however, the doctor was convinced I didn't have a chance. "Hugo, I think this is it," he said one day.

"Foot, I don't think so," my father replied. "That boy could probably walk if you would let him."

I got out of bed, took a couple of steps and fell. But Daddy picked me up and said, "You see, Foot?"

If it hadn't have been for that high-powered nurse who tended the bedpan, took my temperature, fed me every bite of food with his old trademark, "Open up, Son," and personally supervised every sheet and pajama change, I'm sure I wouldn't have made it. It is one reason I have always been confident of his love. Nothing but pure love could have put him on bedpan duty.

While Daddy served in the Senate my brother and I had to transfer into and out of schools in the middle of the year. Each time we transferred, we had to go through the process of establishing ourselves even if we had attended the school before. Most of the time, I managed to get along by using diplomacy—smiling and avoiding anyone who appeared bent on trouble. All went well until one day Daddy told me about a schoolyard, fight he starred in when he was a child. It seems that there was this one overgrown boy who had everyone terrorized. While Hugo was talking to Gertrude White, the town beauty, in the schoolyard the bully hit him from the rear. "I started to depart," said Daddy, "but Gertrude was looking, so I had to do something. I started crying and making noises and ripped into that fella. Well, sir, nobody had ever done that before. He broke and ran, and I ran after, hoping I wouldn't catch up—and I didn't. But after that, everybody beat on that poor bully. He was all bluff, thank the Lord."

This story probably cost me more bruises, cuts and pure humiliation than anything else in my life. When a bully started pushing me around in front of two young ladies, I decided to test Daddy's story. It was one of the most foolish mistakes I ever made. Even though it was a first-grade fight, they had to take me to the infirmary. The guy took me by the hair and knocked my head on the ground, stomped on me, and to add a finishing touch, ground gravel into my face. After one more encounter with another bully, a no-contest fight that took me a good two

weeks to recover from, I decided to leave the bullies to
Daddy.

I caused him a lot of disappointment during my grammar school days. Like most fathers, he wanted his name-
sake to achieve as an extension of himself, I guess, and
this pressure was not good for my confidence or self-
image. In the first place, he was really one heck of a man.
The closer I got, the more apparent this became, and any
comparison eroded whatever confidence I might have had
in myself.

According to today's psychology (and I believe it is
right), a parent should encourage, not discourage, confidence in his child. But Daddy went about raising me just
the opposite way. He felt he had to keep me from becoming conceited, and I used to boil with indignation and
resentment at his criticism of me. This treatment might
have destroyed me had my mother not constantly pointed
out, "Love cares and criticizes. Only someone who believes you have something very special would be concerned that you might become conceited."

Whenever my grades went down after a period of being
extremely high, he would yell at me, "Why do you have
to swoop after you soar!"

It made me cry, and Mama told him, "Darling, how
many fathers have sons that ever soar?"

But when Daddy left she asked me, "Why do you do
it, Son?"

"I don't know," I said. "But whenever I do good, my
friends always say it's because he's who he is. Maybe it's
because I just want to show 'em that even if I'm his son,
I can be one of them—just like everybody else."

He had no mercy on me or Sterling when we fouled up.

There was a time when he became convinced that the funny papers were to blame for our less than perfect grades. So he declared a moratorium: "No reading of the funny papers."

I accepted the edict because I had brought it on. Sterling, however, an inveterate funny paper reader, had on his last report card brought home grades as perfect as the "master" ever had. "Daddy," he said, "I don't think the funny paper ban should apply to me." For whatever reason he had in mind, Daddy said, "I think it should."

So Sterling ran away, and got nearly twenty miles away before he got tired and called Daddy to come and get him.

When he brought Sterling home, Hugo marched him up to the attic, and then came back down and said to me, "Don't you go up there. Sterling cannot come down for a week." I obeyed, but I have always thought this whole performance was one of the dumbest things Daddy ever did.

The frivolous aspects of the newspapers were among his pet gripes then. At that time, I was a great sports fan, and devoured the sports page. He would have people, even newspapermen, call me and ask me sports questions, and I always knew the answers. One day he jumped me good. "Son," he said, "you got the memory and the mind, why won't you put them to learning what counts instead of this sports junk? Why do you have to put that fine mind on that stuff?"

But it was not just sports that Daddy considered frivolous. He thought birthdays were a farce, and would simply give me a dollar to celebrate. Christmas was not his time either. He would mutter about the merchants using it to pressure people into buying stuff they couldn't afford. The same went for Easter, Father's Day, Mother's Day; if he ever got anybody a present on his own, I never heard of it.

Daddy, however, was no spoilsport. He was always able to get tremendous enjoyment out of life, and despite his complaining, he could be a barrel of fun on holidays. The one ceremony, though, that he seemed to enjoy most was making steaks for the whole family. We kids used to love it when he would go to the market and then come home and prepare steaks his own special way. Steaks always meant something special to him. Long before I was born, some doctor had told him that it was necessary for him to eat steak every day in order to preserve his health. Price was always an object, but not when health was involved, and I know that Daddy relished this advice. In bad times as well as good, he had to have steak.

Another thing Daddy enjoyed was music. Not only did he enjoy singing as he walked around the house, but he also had a special knack for picking out simple tunes on the piano, ocarina, harmonica, guitar, or jew's-harp. And he loved to dance. "I don't know the steps they want to it," he would say, "but I know how to step to it," and he would take off to the rhythm, steps eccentric but rhythm-right.

I would never have seen him play the fiddle if I hadn't started an ill-fated series of violin lessons. No sooner had I got it than he asked me for my instrument to see what he could do. He took it, held it loosely away from his chin, and began to play, touching the bow lightly to the strings. The tunes tumbled out as he circled around the room moving in time to the music. Mama and I joined hands and started jumping up and down: "Step around there, darlin'. That's it, circle right, now circle left and spin around—that's it—come on, Son, spin with your mother. That's a boy."

He played for an hour, working up a good sweat, before laying down the fiddle. "I think you'll like it, son," he said, kind of slinking away, as if he were embarrassed because he had been carried away. It was unfortunate that he always seemed ashamed of his musical talent, as if he thought it was too frivolous.

By the fourth grade I had become second in command of the schoolboy patrol at Horace Mann School in D. C., which meant that I had the power to let patrolmen off duty early, station them where I wanted, and control their signals. One day a patrolboy offered me a sandwich when I was checking the posts at lunchtime. I took it and said jokingly in front of a lot of guys and girls, "O.K. You can go off duty early today." Of course, the boy did not, but someone reported the incident to the principal, who reported it to Daddy.

He took me into the living room and said, "Son, it has been reported to me that you took a bribe."

I fell back aghast. "What are you talking about, Daddy?"

"You let a patrolboy off duty at lunchtime for a sandwich."

"I did not."

"Well, it does not matter whether you did or did not—you've got to learn that a leader has to avoid even the appearance of dishonesty. And you've got to be more serious, you can't joke about stuff like that—"

I became so incensed I could not even speak. For weeks

I said nothing to him. I just boiled with hate, because he ended the conversation by saying, "I have suggested to the principal that she put you down to private."

In retaliation I quit the patrol because I felt I had been dealt with in a totally unjustified manner. If it had not been for Mama, I do not think I could ever have been reconciled to Daddy again. But she said it was her fault for making me so playful and full of fun, and this helped ease my bad feelings.

As a boy scout I really disappointed him. I did not want to be one, but he was bound and determined that I should join a troop, and so I did. As I now look back, I think I had a way of escaping things by getting sick. The night of scout meeting I was always ill with one thing or another—a cold, an asthma attack or hay fever. On the award night I attended with Daddy and Mama, I placed dead last in the troop. To this day I can remember Daddy's face when the scoutmaster remarked, "Hugo has been sick a great deal," to justify my ignoble position.

In those days Daddy just could not understand me at all. I loved Henry "Heinie" Manush, the left fielder of the 1933 Washington Senators, and so I saved by carrying the Washington *News* to get a Senator cap with Heinie's number "3" on it. When Daddy saw it he said, "Lord, wouldn't you know my boy would want to be like Heinie Manush instead of Thomas Jefferson."

Once when I was on the school boy patrol, he came by my post at Cathedral Avenue and 45th Street as he was driving to work and happened to hear me yelling at the top of my lungs to a guy across the street. My heart sank as I saw the car stop. He told me to get in, then turned and took me home and made me wash my mouth out with

soap. I said through my tears, "Daddy, what did I do?"
"You were cussing like a fool trying to be a big man.
Your mother and I won't tolerate that cussing in or out-
side the house. It's time you learned that."

Daddy used to embarrass me to death telling stories on
me that I certainly would never tell on my son. He would
say at a party where I could hear, "My son, Hugo, made
us go to see the first-grade play at Oyster School. We
thought from what he said he was the star. When we got
down there, we watched the whole play, but we didn't see
him. When it was all over, he said to me, 'How'd I do,
Pop?' I told him I didn't see him. Then he said, 'Well, Pop,
you saw the horse.' 'Yeah,' I said; then Hugo said, 'Well,
Pop, I was the hind legs.' " I wanted to kill him every time
he told that story. Then I would hear him go on with
another: "Hugo always wanted me to run over every boy
he saw on a bicycle. Then one day he saw this boy, and,
quite concerned, he said, 'Pop, don't run over that boy.'
I said, 'Why not—you always want me to run over all the
boys riding bicycles.' Hugo said, 'That's my bicycle, Pop.
I lent it to him.' "

He insisted that we build good habits in the small
things of life, such as automatically snapping off a light
whenever you leave a room. "It makes life so much easier
later on." There was nothing I did that couldn't be improved upon, from table manners to toilet habits. Once
when I was in the bathroom he burst in and said, "Son,
they can hear you all over the house. When a man wee-
wees in the bathroom, he has got to turn the water on and
run it hard so as to cover up the other noise."

There are many ways to express love, but perhaps none
is more profound than caring, even when it takes distaste-

ful forms, such as criticizing, carping and insisting upon perfection. Of course, only one who is beyond reproach can get away with loving in this fashion, else the loved one is likely to say, "Look at yourself, buddy, then tell me what's wrong with me." But, somehow, no matter how angry he made me, I never felt like saying that to Daddy.

From the Senate
to the Supreme Court

ও৳

Although my father loved the power and hard work that go with being a senator, much of what a senator needs to do to stay in office vexed him. Chitchat bored him to death, and even though he was very good at it, he had to force himself to mingle in a crowd and shake hands to win votes.

Job-seekers always plague a senator, and Daddy found it especially hard to deal with them. The ruined men who came to him during the depression broke his heart. One day a man he greatly respected came to him and said, "Hugo, you are my last hope. If I can't get a job through you, I am just going to have to dispose of myself and feed the family with the proceeds of the insurance." Sorrowfully Daddy had to tell him he had no job for him. The next morning when Daddy picked up the paper, he read that the man had jumped from a building in Birmingham and killed himself. He cried and said, "I couldn't help him. I couldn't help him."

Probably the most important thing to a senator is an

executive secretary who can relieve him of much of the day-to-day dealings with people. Unfortunately for my father, he picked the wrong man for his first one—Hugh Grant. Hugh had been a popular teacher at Auburn and had many friends in Alabama. Not long after he assumed his duties, however, he began to lose the common touch. "The fella has started referring to himself as Dr. Hugh Grant," Daddy said, mimicking the phony British accent that Hugh Grant had taken on. As Hugh lost the common touch, Daddy had to take over more and more of the secretary's duties or lose his job. So he looked for a way out that would not hurt Hugh's feelings.

On a visit to President Roosevelt one day, Daddy told him of his problem. FDR said, "Hugo, I believe I can help you. What do you think the Doctor would feel about becoming my ambassador to the court of King Zog of Albania?"

"Mr. President," Hugo replied, "does the job require the title of Doctor and that one appear in a swallow-tailed coat and a top hat?"

"All three are essential to this important post, Hugo."

"Mr. President," said Daddy, "I believe you have found yourself the ideal man."

After Dr. Grant departed for Albania, Hugo's nephew, Hollis Black, became his executive secretary. Hollis performed ideally, and made each constituent feel important. But even though he was a tremendous help to my father, making his workload lighter, Daddy still yearned to have more time to reflect upon important ideas, especially those relating to the country's economy.

Fortunately, things fell into place for Daddy. In the summer of 1937, when he was fifty-one years old, the announcement came. I was fifteen at the time and I remember hearing it over the radio. "President Roosevelt today sent to the Senate the appointment of Hugo L. Black to the Supreme Court."

Daddy had been raising so much hell about watching our pennies that I remember being very excited that now finally we would have much more money, his salary going from $10,000 to $25,000. That was in the days when the conservatives were in the Supreme Court, the liberals in the Congress. A day would come when the situation would be reversed—the liberals on the Court, the conservatives in Congress. Then, since the Constitution gave Congress the power to fix the salaries of Supreme Court Justices, the conservatives in Congress would do their best to chastise the Justices by using this power against them. But there was no way that kind of power play would ever make Daddy more conservative. "These nuts," he would say, "think everybody does whatever they do for money. That's what I've been telling you, Son. If you do the right, you've got to be able to take a little hardship now and then."

Hugo's nomination caused a small furor because of his previous connection with the Klan. Supposedly, even FDR was surprised to learn of this, but he certainly did not want to withdraw the nomination. In the midst of this public uproar, we were all treated to a pleasant visit with the President.

On a Sunday afternoon we arrived at the White House and were admitted into a small study; the first thing I noticed was the model sailing ships on the tables. FDR was sitting on the couch talking with his secretary Missy LeHand.

"Josephine," he said as he saw us enter, "you sit down beside me," and he put his arm around Mama. "Come here, boys, shake hands with me." Sterling and I did.

"Josephine," he said, "you are beautiful. Missy, why don't you take the Justice and the rest of them out in the garden. Josephine, you stay with me."

Mama said, "Oh, Mr. President—"

"I'm serious," he said. "Don't think I'm harmless, just because I'm crippled."

"Mr. President," I said, "how do you get all these ship models in these bottles?"

"You blow the bottle up round the ships," he said.

I looked very closely. "But how do you get this bottle shaped around it, sir?"

"Well, there is a mold."

Mama said, "Aw, Mr. President, tell him the truth."

The President looked at Mama, then to me, and said, "Well, Hugo, the model is collapsed when it goes in. You slip it in that way, then pull it up and it stays."

I looked at Mama, not really believing the President. She did not really know how it was done, but she knew the level from the slant. "That's right, honey, that's the way it's done."

Then Sterling said, "Mr. President, can I have your autograph?"

"Many times as you want it, son, if—"

"If what?" said Sterling.

"If you promise not to sell it in the near future."

"I promise," said Sterling.

Missy LeHand produced a pad and a pen and gave it to the President.

Mama said, "Why not in the near future?"

"Because," he said, "I want it to bring twenty-five thousand dollars. If he keeps it long enough it will. I want little Hugo to have one too. But, I want them to guard these autographs with their lives."

He presented us both with a felicitation in his handwriting, followed by his signature. I am ashamed to say that we both lost these autographs and a bottle with a ship in it that he gave us on that occasion. Such is the callousness of two boys growing up in the shadow of the great figures of history.

In the next few weeks as my father waited for Senate confirmation, he got a bad rap on the Ku Klux Klan.

During this time, Mama became depressed, and she told Daddy, "I'm afraid they are going to get you."

He said, "No, they are not."

Seeing this had not calmed Mama, he said, "Darling, it would be much better for you if they got me. I'd just have to go out and earn two hundred and fifty thousand dollars a year, and I'd get to stay home a lot more the way you want me to."

As far as my own feelings about this go, all I can say is that I lived with him and close to him for fifty years, and I never noticed in him even a mite of feeling that one man differed from another on any standard other than individual excellence. But if the black man was not as good as the Irishman as an individual, or the Italian was not as good as the black man, you could not change his bad feelings about this person by saying, "Well, he's black," or "But he's Italian." With Hugo you were on your own every minute. The rich, the classy, the aristocrats never got from him one ounce of respect simply because of their position, and neither could a man use the fact that he was poor or a member of a minority group to justify bad character traits. Usually, he compared you with himself, and you came out the loser. Compared to his own self-discipline, he thought you were too flabby. Compared to his own motivation and goal orientation, you had no "self starter." Compared to his own sense of schedule, you would probably be called a "procrastinator." And so it went.

The Ku Klux Klan and Daddy, so far as I could tell, only had one thing in common. He suspected the Catholic Church. He used to read all of Paul Blanshard's books exposing power abuse in the Catholic Church. He thought the popes and bishops had too much power and property. He resented the fact that rental property owned by the Church was not taxed; he felt they got most of their revenue from the poor and they did not return enough of it. But even then his favorite district judge was a man who had been a bishop's lawyer. Defender of a bishop's property, defender of the Church's exemption— but to Daddy this man was one of "the best district judges in America, because he is one of the best human beings in America."

I am Justice Black's son, and, of course, I am prejudiced in his favor. Yet I think anyone can see how a young man in his particular circumstances at that particular time would be tempted to become a member: he needed it to be what he was—the best trial lawyer in the South. I am certain that he never participated in or agreed with any of the Klan's violent, lawless methods of promoting their beliefs, and that the thought of even his minimal involvement must have caused him some pangs of conscience.

While he and Mama were in Europe for a few weeks

following his nomination, their vacation was practically ruined by reporters. Following his usual practice, he said nothing but "No comment." I suppose he did this out of a combination of paranoia and the knowledge that newspaper reporters write too fast under too much pressure to be accurate. I thought this was a mistake, because the rare times he did talk with them he was great. You could tell they loved him and thought him brilliant. When I so informed him, he replied, "Yes, the reporters are all right. But they aren't in control—they will get me on the editorial page. The owners are after me." He was right. In those days, most publishers had little use for a man of the people.

The worst thing he should have had to endure in his lifetime for joining the Ku Klux Klan is the story I used to tell on him when I introduced him to speak: "Ladies and gentlemen, I give you Justice Black. When he first went on the U.S. Supreme Court they talked about him as a man who went around in a white robe scaring black people. Now they talk about him as a man who goes about in a black robe scaring white people."

Teenage Days

Right after Daddy got on the Court, I was in the middle of those awkward adolescent years, and it was a period when Daddy was really down on me. He used to say, "Son, stop stalking around the house trying to find a way to waste time. I'm working and I don't have time to waste talking about nothing. Go upstairs and study. Do something."

"But Daddy," I'd say, "I got the grades."

"Yeah, I know, but I don't know how. Go on upstairs and get to work. Don't play the records—work!"

I'd go up and then decide to take a shower. Whenever I did, water leaked through the ceiling to the second floor. I would be singing, happy as a lark—to Mama, it was music from the stars—but all of a sudden, up from the hall on the second floor would come his voice: "Son, Good Lord, what are you doing!" I'd pretend not to hear. Then he would bust into the bathroom, coughing and flipping at the steam with his hands. "Good Lord, you're steaming open the seams and the plaster, cut it off. Cut it off. The plaster's coming out downstairs. Get out." I would turn off the water. "What's the matter, Pop?"

"Son, pull the curtain around."

"I did."

"No, you didn't. If you did, it wouldn't do like this." And he would work the curtain around while I stood there all soaped up. While he worked, he would say, "Son, you are shower-crazy."

"No, I'm not, Daddy, I—"

"I know—you haven't had one since between now and after school. That's the last time some plaster fell. Face reality, son. You're shower-crazy."

"Daddy, I'm all soaped up, can I wash off the soap?"

"All right. But be careful. Plaster costs money—you know I don't have a lot of it." Years later, however, we found the leaking wasn't my fault—the pipes just weren't fitted right.

One day, Daddy let me take our Oldsmobile 88 to school. I had been bragging about the power of Daddy's Oldsmobile to a friend of mine, whom Daddy regarded as a nitwit spoiled by his banker father. That afternoon, my friend challenged me to a race on the Mt. Vernon Highway, and I accepted. He and I ripped away as soon as we hit the highway. I had him by ten car lengths when I spotted a mouse-colored '36 Plymouth doubling back on the highway. Mama had a car that looked just like that, but there was a man at the wheel. Could it be? I thought —No. No way. And I kept my foot on the floor.

That evening as I walked in the door, he was sitting in the chair in the hall. Mama was playing a sad song on the piano. He stuck out his hand. "Give me those keys, Son," he said. "Son, that car is too powerful for your brain. Your buddy," he said, shaking his head. "I told you. Keep fooling with that fool and you'll get killed." He never let me drive that Oldsmobile again, and somehow after that day, I just lost my taste for speed.

We thought that Daddy was mighty tough on us about clothes. Before shingles wrecked his feet and made him chase around all over the place for a comfortable pair of shoes, he used to buy about one pair every ten years that he had resoled while he waited. He was so frugal that whenever Sterling or I wanted an extra pair of shoes, he would say, "You are shoe-crazy."

He honestly believed that one pair of shoes, one pair of pants, one shirt, one sweater, one coat, two pairs of socks and two sets of underwear were all that a young teenage fellow needed. Fortunately for me and Sterling, our sizes were the same in our late teens, so we could trade clothes. Of course, it made everybody at our high school think we were twins, but that was O.K. A change of outfits is nice. When we complained, Daddy said, "You got to learn to live simply, boys, or you will be slaves, you'll be tempted to sell out your ideas and principles. I want you to learn to live simply."

Daddy had an idea in those days that I always ordered the most expensive thing in a restaurant. One night we went to Hogate's in Washington, D. C., with Senator and Mrs. Lister Hill. Daddy looked down the menu and said to me, "I suppose you'll want the most expensive item as usual. Here, it's the combination seafood platter."

Although I never really chose food because it was the most expensive, I did enjoy seafood, so I said, "Sure, Daddy."

When it came, the amount was monstrous. I ate about

three-fourths of it and stopped. Then Daddy said, "Eat the rest of it."

"I don't want it."

"I don't care. Eat it. If you order the expensive stuff, you eat it."

Tears came down my cheeks as I started to finish it off. I felt very sick, but I would not give him the satisfaction of knowing it. I ate the whole damn thing, then when he was deep in conversation, I slipped out to the men's room and got very sick. I admit that I would have liked to kill him that night.

Luckily, I did have an ally in those days. When my sister Jo-Jo was born in 1933, Annie, also known as Madam Five-by-Five, came to work for us. Annie was good at spoiling me, and she would always feed me well to "stouten" me up. Once when we were eating dinner, Annie came in to announce that she had just decided to name her latest grandchild Hugo. Daddy said, "Annie, I appreciate that. That is one of the nicest compliments I ever had."

"Judge," she said, "that boy's not named after you. He's named after little Hugo."

Whenever Daddy would jump on me for not making my bed, Annie would come up to me afterwards and say, "Don't pay no attention to him. I'll make it up for you. You've got to be raised a gentleman and a gentleman don't make his bed. You're either going to have a servant make it up for you when you grow up, or a woman—it's bound to happen—one or the other. You leave your room to me."

Daddy, of course, would have scolded Annie if he heard her say this. He had always drummed it into us that it was important to be a "plain fella." After dinner, even at a friend's house, he would jump up and help with the dishes. Mama once told me she was afraid he might do this at an affair of state.

When I started playing tennis with him, he was in his fifties and I in my teens. He had kept in shape and had played tennis for a long time. Although he had played some real experts, he would never accept defeat after losing a match, but would always insist on playing again until the other guy either quit from sheer exhaustion or was beaten.

When Daddy played with me he knew how to keep himself cool when he flubbed one, and I did not. When he dinked it to me I would slug it back, and when it went out I would howl, throw my racket, whine, and stomp. He would say to me, "Son, that's no good, now stop. Serve."

When we met friends, he would brag about how he beat me. Although he could afford it, he never had me take lessons. At that time he really never tried to improve my game. He just enjoyed telling everybody, "I can whip my boy who is only seventeen."

Since I am his son, I got tired of this. I had friends my own age who were good tennis players. They gave me tips, and I practiced and practiced. Then I played him. I was still not much good really, but I stomped him, beat him one set after another until he said, "Son, we'll play again tomorrow."

I never asked him to play again. After that, we just "practiced" or played doubles, so there was no more direct competition between us. And to his credit, since he always rated the players in our doubles games, he always rated me many notches ahead of him.

In checkers, however, it never changed. He whipped me

good right up to the last game we played. And he loved it.

Daddy was wrong, I believe, in making me feel so bad about my adolescent acne. He had never had a sign of it, and so he kept saying to me, "I can't see how you could have it, Son, I never did." He treated it as some sort of disease to run away from. Jo-Jo, my little sister, picked up his habit and threw it at me. Every morning she reported on the state of my pimpled face, and he encouraged her. Mama, though, would always interrupt to say, "I had some, lots more than Hugo has." That, of course, soothed my feelings despite Daddy's harping on the painful subject.

No matter what high grades I made in my teenage days, they were never good enough for him. About every other semester, I used to "break the bank" by getting all A's and winning highest honors. He never remarked about that. He only talked about the one before that when I had goofed up. He reminded me that he had gotten "perfect grades" all through school. It did no good to "streak," you had to be consistent in this life. He would tell me, "If you don't do better, you'll wind up a ditch digger." Then he would remind me for the hundredth time of John Densler Black, the son of Uncle Orlando, who went from laziness in his schoolwork to drinking, to gambling, to dope—and to the grave before he was thirty-five.

In many ways, he was a Spartan. Even though he loved to smoke, he quit forever as soon as it was determined that the habit was unhealthy. And he had not an ounce of respect for anyone who couldn't quit cold turkey like him. To make sure he would always be in good shape, he had paid some guy to give him a series of exercises, and he took them regularly from as far back as I can remember until he was seventy years old. How Sterling and I hated those exercises. But it made no difference. We had to take them with him too.

"All right, boys," he would holler first thing in the morning, "seven o'clock."

In the midst of our workout before breakfast, he would get me and Sterling to stand on his stomach to prove how tough it was. Then he would stand up and invite us to pop him in the stomach with our fists. Then back to our exercises. Finally, after about a half-hour of this routine, he would say, "All right, boys. Let's take our cold shower."

Then all three of us would have to go into an ice-cold shower for about five minutes. "Man—this will make you feel good, boys," he would say.

"That's great for your heart, boys. Now watch this— you got to towel off good."

How Sterling and I hated that cold shower. But one day, after reading a magazine article, Daddy called up our family doctor to verify its contents. "Boys," he said to us that night, "we can't take any more cold showers. Dr. Dickens says they are bad for your heart." We tried not to show our disappointment.

Both Dr. Foster and my father believed that prunes were essential to health. Because Daddy was such a prune lover, it was sometimes necessary for him to spring from the breakfast table and retreat rapidly for more intimate parts of the house. When the seizure struck him, he would throw down his knife and fork and speed off, somewhere along the line saying, "Shoo-shoo-excuse me."

One day after he had gotten out of sight, I sprang up

saying, "Shoo-shoo-excuse me," to the howling delight of Mama and Sterling and Jo-Jo, slinging my feet out the way he did, and whistling "All Policemen Have Big Feet" —to the tune of "London Bridge"—his trademark song. It was Daddy to a T.

That morning of all mornings, he had had a remission of the seizure before it drove to its ultimate conclusion. He saw me as he returned to the room, and looked at me in disgust.

"Son," he said, "You have a deadly talent. Mimicry is a talent, but it's deadly. It makes enemies. It's easy to draw laughs at somebody else's expense. You got to use it so that you don't make fun of other people. Come on upstairs. I want to show you in this book. This isn't something I just made up. I think it's Marcus Aurelius—"

Jo-Jo, Sterling and Mama sat solemnly watching as I was led away to be shown in the classics the deadliness of my alleged talent.

Teacher

As a teacher, Daddy could get things through my skull when nobody else could. Whenever he decided one of us kids was not learning our lessons properly, he would simply take it upon himself to teach us. While I was in elementary school he spent many hours tutoring me in spelling. With him in the teacher's chair, you never lost your concentration. Maybe you wanted to kill him or maybe you started crying—but your mind always stayed on the subject.

It was a long time after he made me into a near-perfect speller before he had time to teach me again. But the time came—just before Roosevelt appointed him to the Supreme Court. I had gotten the idea I was a mathematical moron. He said he did not think I was—that, instead, my difficulty was a character defect: "I am sick and tired of hearing you whine you can't learn math." I was then about fifteen years old, and he told me we would do algebra, which was what I was taking the next year.

"Son, we will master it."

"Daddy, I can't," I said.

Just as he did whenever I said those words, he exploded: "Son, you can—how many times I told you not to say 'can't.' We'll start tomorrow."

Next day at breakfast, he put my book down in front of me and said, "O.K., Son, from eight A.M. until twelve noon is your working time. I'll make the assignments. Here's the first one." And from that moment on I worked hard every morning during the summer, practicing over and over again all the problems to make sure I really knew the book. When fall arrived, for the first time in my life I led my math class. Despite the delicious joy of being at the top, I can still feel today the pain of what I had to go through to get there.

It wasn't until I had graduated from the University of Alabama that he again decided to teach me. I had been accepted at a number of law schools, and, naturally, considered myself quite the learned young man. One day shortly after returning to D.C., I said smugly to Daddy, "Do you realize I have gotten an A all the way through college on any subject having to do with writing?"

He shook his head and replied, "Son, that's a sad commentary—you haven't lit a flick of smoke. You are lazy. I have decided I won't contribute any money for you to go to law school. You just won't work."

"Daddy," I said, "Daddy, good night, you can't do better than A. What in the world do I have to do to please you?"

I stomped out of the study. Sitting in my bedroom, I had time to cool off and think it over. I knew it was important that I regain my self-control in order to see the situation in the proper light. If I hadn't stomped out of the study, I might have been able to reason with him. I remembered how self-control was such a big issue with Daddy and what he had told me once: "Self-control didn't come easy for me, Son. I had to practice it—pick something I liked and quit it. Why," he said with a twinkle in his eyes, "I used to give up women for certain periods of time just to see if I could. And I always could."

After a while, I was in a more rational frame of mind. I decided to go back downstairs and see if there was some way to deal with him.

"Is there anything I can do to change your mind?" I said, after walking back into the study.

"Work with me this summer and do just what I say."

At first I felt he did not really mean what he said, but I was not sure. Looking him hard in the eye, I said, "Daddy, I can't please you. You're just plain unfair. But I'll think about it."

I stewed around all night about my decision. One minute I felt like packing up my clothes and moving out. The next minute I would say to myself, "What other twenty-four-year-old has an opportunity to get trained by this kind of a guy?"

I talked it over with Mama. She agreed with me that Daddy had not put the matter to me very nicely and that perhaps his judgment about my past lack of intellectual industry was wrong. But she thought he had presented me with a very rare opportunity. Men of his position, superior intellect, energy and wisdom just did not take the time to fill in the weak points of a young man's education. And she reminded me, "Honey, you have been sick quite a bit of each school year and you have missed a lot. I think you ought to do it."

Next morning I walked into the study and sat down in

the chair by the desk. Daddy was sitting in his usual spot reading. "O.K., Daddy," I said. "I'm ready, what's first?"

He put down his book and picked up another. "Here, take this upstairs and read as much as you can. Then we'll talk about it tonight. What we'll do is this: weekdays you'll work all day after our exercises, with an hour off for lunch. In the evenings we'll talk about what you've worked on. You can take the weekends off and go out Friday and Saturday nights. That will be our routine. Things work by habit, you know. I want you to develop good work habits this summer—steady ones, not streaky ones." I took the book upstairs. It was Holmes's *Common Law.*

That night after supper, he took the book from me and asked me what part I had read. I showed him. Right off he said, "What is a tort?"

"I don't know."

"Hmm," he said. "What is conversion?"

"Conversion is when you change from one thing to another."

He closed the book and threw it at me.

"Good Lord, it's worse than I thought. You're either too lazy to use the dictionary or you don't know how. You're not ready to discuss anything. Don't ever come in here again telling me you've read something when you don't even know what key words mean. Now spend the rest of the night learning all the words you passed over that might as well be ink spots for all they mean to you."

Old as I was, I felt like crying, and when I stood up I really felt like slugging him. But instead, I picked up *Webster's Second International Dictionary,* which he always kept in the study, and went to work.

"Daddy," I said the next night, "I didn't realize there

were so many words I was blank on or just plain wrong about."

"Something else you got to remember, Son. Something like 'convert' has more than one meaning—the meaning you gave me last night and the meaning somewhere between 'steal' and 'take' that it has in common law. If a word you've seen and know looks out of context, always look it up to see if there's a meaning other than the one you know."

Each night while I was struggling through *Common Law* we would go up after dinner to the study and he would start in on me.

"What does Holmes mean by 'common law'? "

"Law that does not come from a statute or a constitution."

"Where does common law come from then?"

"From a prior decision."

"Where does that prior decision come from?"

"A dead judge from another generation."

"Where did the judge get it?"

"Well, he just knew it was the right thing."

"How did he know it any better than the last judge who had to decide the problem?"

"Well, he didn't."

"Why does the last judge have to follow it?"

"Because that's the way it is. You got to follow the law. You got to be able to predict the consequences of certain conduct. You got to follow precedent, Daddy."

"Do the judges always do it?"

"The conscientious good ones do."

"Didn't Holmes say the common law evolved to meet the needs of changing times?"

"Sure, Holmes said that. It's the genius of the common law."

"Who brings about this evolution?"

"Why, the judges."

"If that's so, don't we owe the genius of the common law to the bad judges?"

"Aw, Daddy, of course not."

"Well, you said the good judges don't change anything. They just follow precedent so people will know the consequence of their conduct."

That's the way it went.

There followed Benjamin Cardozo's *Judicial Process,* Karl Llewellyn's *Bramble Bush,* Kenneth Crawford's *Quest for Law* and, to balance things out, Fred Rodell's *Woe Unto You Lawyers.* Within two weeks, I was so fascinated I could hardly wait to get up to the study for more discussion.

As he questioned me, I never made an answer that he did not contradict with a counterproposition, and although this was initially confusing I would become so stimulated that I frequently could not go to sleep. Sometimes after we had been in the study for hours on end, Mama would come in and say, "Are you fellas mad?"

"Now, darling," Daddy would say, "I am just clearing this young mind of error."

When I finished John Stuart Mill's *Logic,* he commented to me that night: "Son, you can compare anything with something else or you can distinguish it from anything else. It's all a matter of degree. That's most what the law is—comparing and distinguishing. You get to be a good lawyer when you can judge the degree of comparison or difference that means something."

Another night we were discussing "warranties of title."

"What's the significance of a warranty of title?"

"Well, Daddy, if the title turns out to be bad and you lose the house, you can sue the guy who sold it to you and make him pay you the value of the house."

"Do you think that you should always insist on a warranty deed?"

"Sure, only a nut would take a house without a warranty deed."

"What if it was a good bargain and the abstract didn't show any defects and the seller didn't have anything but he just wouldn't give a warranty deed—would you refuse to buy the house?"

"Why, certainly, Daddy, why not?"

"Good night, Son, you are completely impractical. What difference does it make whether the fella warrants title. He doesn't have anything, so there wouldn't be anything you could do with a warranty deed you couldn't do with a quit claim deed anyhow—you can't get blood out of a turnip. You've got to learn how to be practical. Never insist on something because of a beautiful legal concept unless it makes a difference."

For a period of a week or so, he drilled me on syllogisms and drawing inferences, making me dream up all kinds of examples. Then we started in on Aristotle's *Topics.* It was boring and tough, but with Daddy helping to clarify some of its more obscure passages, I did finally understand how the book lays out usable tools for thinking and argument.

Toward the end of summer, I began to get restless, particularly in the Aristotle cycle. It was the longest sustained period of concentrated intellectual activity I had ever endured. I began to sneak in a nap or two upstairs in the daytime—but not for long. One afternoon I woke up and to my great dismay saw him standing over me shaking his head in disgust. I jumped up. He just looked at me and said, "Go to the ant, thou sluggard, and consider his ways."

I got right back to work and kept at it until by the end of the summer I was ready to head for Yale Law School. I still did not know whether he would help me financially. Then finally one night he said, "Son, I'm going to send you to law school. You will do all right—better each year. The other fellas will be ahead of you for a while, but you'll catch up. You're going to make a lawyer. I am sure of it."

From that day forward, I had confidence in myself. If I could satisfy him, I could make it as a lawyer. I knew it had to be. Sentiment just could not make him say something like that.

I was not the only one he spent time teaching. Daddy had a very special relationship with his law clerks, which resembled his relationship with me. He never felt that he needed a clerk, and he never accepted the work of a clerk without going over it again himself and checking it, for he considered his work to be a personal job which demanded a consistent philosophy over the years. Daddy hired law clerks only because this gave him an opportunity to send an apostle of his "views" into a community. If he could, he would always hire young people from the South, who he believed might be persuaded to return there. He thought it was his duty to teach each clerk and build up any weaknesses in their intellectual ability, character or even personality. He genuinely cared about them.

He expected his clerks to criticize his work without

mercy and expected them to test every statement, fact, and argument he ever wrote. Not that he would not bristle and fight back—he always would. But he loved the contest. Although I never heard him acknowledge that a clerk was right and that he was wrong, many times he accepted without comment the suggestion of a clerk.

No clerk escaped criticism. "You waste time talking about nothing," he'd tell one. Or, "You had better study the ways of a Southern woman. You just make everybody mad." Or, to another, "Take this grammar book and start doing the exercises." But somehow he managed to become a hero to most of his clerks. Each clerk would work on that term's major opinions, staying with him late into the night, suggesting language changes, restructuring, questioning, fighting. And each one left feeling that he had contributed something to the career of a very important justice, and he usually had.

Each of the clerks eventually became almost like members of our family, and you might say there has always been some good-natured sibling rivalry among them and Sterling and myself over which of the "sons" was the favorite. All of us like to think of ourselves as the favored one, much as each of his old Alabama senatorial constituents believed he was his "best friend." But if Daddy was a big enough man to give us so much of himself, I see no harm in each of us considering himself the favorite.

Women Are
Just Better than Men

My father never understood what Rex Harrison meant in
My Fair Lady when he sang "Why can't a woman be more
like a man?" He believed that a good woman is something
completely distinct from a man, and that is why a good
woman beats what a man is by a long way. A woman who
behaved in what he regarded as a masculine way made
him uneasy, for he believed that a real woman cultivated
an appearance and personal ways calculated to attract and
please men and serve as the hub of a family.

On many occasions he said to me, "Son, women are just
nicer than men." Or, "Son, a good man will sometimes
hurt people and be very selfish, but a good woman will
never hurt anybody and generally will dedicate her life to
helping other people."

He could idealize a woman to the point where he believed she was nearly perfect. So strong was his prefer-
ence for women that a sensitive male who loved him
might feel hurt. As deeply as I know he loved me, sometimes I wonder. When his book *A Constitutional Faith* was

published, he dedicated it to his mother, Mama, Jo-Jo and Elizabeth (his second wife), but never mentioned me or Sterling.

According to him, scholarship should never play too big a role in a woman's life. When it came time for my sister Jo-Jo to go to college, Daddy tried to steer her away from coed, intellectual Swarthmore to Sweet Briar, the school Mama had attended, which Daddy believed to be the finest place in the world for the education of a woman. I was proud of Jo-Jo when she stuck up for her rights and insisted upon Swarthmore.

Although he tried to be charitable about it, he would sometimes by reflex action wrinkle up his face, as if he had eaten something sour, when forced into contact with a woman very ugly in physical appearance. Fat in a woman literally revolted him, and no favorite of his could go to fat without his telling them "in confidence" what was happening to them.

From the time she was born, he always had a warm regard for my first cousin Virginia "Tilla" Darr. When she was a little girl she used to cling to him, literally wrapping herself around him. "Man, that Tilla is going to be a real woman. Pretty as she can be and she's got a way with men." After Tilla became a college student, she came to visit him one day. He was sitting in the chair behind his desk in the study when Tilla walked in with me. I saw him fall back in his chair and his face twist as if he smelled something horrible.

"Son, please leave if you don't mind," he said. "I'd like to talk to Tilla privately."

When I left and the door to the study was shut, he said, "Good Lord, Tilla, you are too fat. How did you let yourself get in that condition?"

That very day Tilla went on a diet and to this day maintains the beautiful physical appearance Daddy always believed she could have.

In his attitude towards women, however, Daddy tended to be something of a Spaniard—a woman was either all good or all bad. He would see a beautiful young girl in a mini-skirt with a well-filled-out sweater walking down the street and say, "Look at that, Son. Look at that. Man, what do you think she's after? I'll tell you something, she is going to find it too."

Once a good friend was staying with me and invited his girlfriend from out of town to our house to play tennis. Afterwards, we all planned to go out along with my girlfriend for drinks, dinner and dancing. Just before we left, Daddy called me into the study and shut the door for a confidential chat. "Son," he said, "if you value your friendship, you better change your plans. That girl came here to see you. She is made for men, and if you get out there with them, you two are going to run off by yourselves sure as I'm talking to you. And when you do, you're going to lose a friend and a regular girl."

"Aw, Daddy, you don't know what you're talking about. I'm not interested in her, and she isn't interested in me."

"You better watch. It's like two live wires jumping around, working toward each other."

Later the next day, he said to me, "Well, I guess you noticed. When you finally got in, your friend had already come back and packed up and left." He shook his head and said "Uh-uh-uh," and walked off.

I do not know the source of his knowledge about this type of woman, but I do know that he was thirty-four years old before he married, which gave him plenty of time for experiences with women. Although he never told me anything about his method of operation, I did see him swing into action in behalf of a friend of mine, John Butler, who was at the house one day playing tennis with me, Sterling and my father. After we finished playing, we were all sitting around and John kept talking about calling this girl up for a date. He would reach for the phone, but then would not pick it up.

Daddy finally said, "John, just pick up the telephone and call her. Don't be bashful."

"Aw, it's too late, Judge, she'll already have a date."

"What's her number?"

John gave it to him. Daddy reached over and picked up the telephone. "Is Jean there?" Then he said, "Jean, you don't know me, but I know of you. I have been sitting here with some fellows who have been talking about you. They say you have a voice like soft music and I wanted to hear for myself. I can tell you, they are right."

Pause.

"Who am I? Well, that doesn't make any difference. Important thing is I got a young fellow here by the name of John Butler who wanted to ask you for a date but was afraid you'd turn him down."

Pause.

"You're going to hang up if I don't tell my name. Aw, you wouldn't do that, but I'll tell you anyhow. I'm Justice Black."

Pause.

"Yes, the Supreme Court Justice."

Pause.

"Yes, I really am. Here, let me get you John. He's just dying to talk to you. I'm going to get him to bring you over here someday to see us. Goodbye, Jean. Here's John."

John took the telephone giggling.

"It really is Justice Black."

Daddy was always very skeptical about prominent old men who married young women, and he would laugh when he read about a well-known man in his eighties fathering a child. "I wonder how old the next-door neighbor is," he would say.

Despite his apparently easy way with women, Daddy never really had the confidence he should have had in his ability to hold his own woman. Although he idealized Mama and put her on a pedestal with women saints, he believed that every man in the world was looking at her, and to his everlasting discredit, he was never really as sure as he should have been that she was not looking back. The jealous streak traced directly back to the big gap between his and my mother's ages. He never could get it through his head that a man so much older could hold a woman like her, who undoubtedly did appeal strongly to men her own age.

Hugo could not stand seeing a woman whom he regarded as charming and attractive without a man. Lucylle, the daughter of his oldest brother Lee, lost her husband while she was still a very attractive woman. A year or so after her husband's death, Lucylle came to visit the family. Almost as soon as she arrived, Daddy took her into the study for one of his confidential talks.

"Lucylle, you are far too attractive to be without a man. But Sylacanga, where you live, is too small for proper exposure. You've got to get into an urban area."

"Uncle Hugo, I just can't do that, I'm making too much money as a real estate broker."

"Well, then, if you're making all that money, you'll have to get the exposure some other way. How about one of those Caribbean cruises?"

He was even less of a gay liberationist than he was a woman's libber, and his feelings on this subject were very intense. Although he admired Socrates in many ways, he thought sexual love should be confined to a man and a woman. A case he had when he was police court judge in Birmingham sums up his attitude pretty well.

"This fella had charged another fella with beating him up. The one charged admitted that he beat the stuffing out of the one who swore out the warrant, but said, 'Judge, sir, this fella made advances to me.' I took one look at the other fella's face and said, 'Is that so?' He just dropped his head. So on my own, I threw out the charges and found the pervert guilty of disorderly conduct and gave him the maximum sentence. That kind of thing will destroy a society, Son."

Maybe because of that same feeling, maybe for some other reason, he was always very reserved in his physical contact with the males he loved best. So far as physical demonstrations are concerned, he and I limited ourselves to handshakes. I never embraced him or kissed him on the cheek, because I knew that such demonstrations of affection between man and man made him uncomfortable. Toward the end, however, I would feel so much affection when I would first see him that I used to put one arm around him and pat him on the far shoulder the way Spanish men greet each other. He never objected to that.

I, of course, didn't subscribe to all of Daddy's sentiments about women and sex, but yet, my father did have a lot to do with the way I felt about the woman I eventually married. In a way, although I wouldn't have admitted it at the time, you could say that it was a craving for approval from my parents that was in part responsible for the most wonderful thing that happened to me: my marriage.

My cousin Ann Durr had been trying for some time to get me interested in her friend Graham Hobson, and arranged a meeting. I thought she was interesting all right, but I wasn't able to get around to doing anything about it because of other relationships that took up what little spare time I had.

The next time Ann arranged a meeting between us was at a friend's home on Seminary Hill. Mama was sick, but Daddy and I went along anyway. Graham was there, looking stunning that night, her large black eyes set in a beautiful oval face. Her voice sounded like music. I played up to her shamelessly, and she seemed to be reacting well. As I showed off, Daddy, much to my surprise, fed me lines, suggested stories for me to tell, acts for me to go into, and otherwise played my straight man. Never before or since have I upstaged him so with his encouragement and consent.

On the way home in the car, he said to me, "Son, I can tell you really like that girl. Lord, but she is beautiful— smart as a whip too."

"Yeah, Daddy, I hear she is a very fine person."

"She appears to be."

"I think I'm going to ask her out, Daddy."

"I'm not sure she'll go out with you, Son. Don't be hurt if she won't. But I'll tell you something, that woman has got it. If she takes a notion to marry you, she will, and you won't even know what happened."

"You don't think she'll do that, do you, Daddy? You trying to scare me off?"

"Son, I'll just be honest with you. I don't know whether you can get a woman of that quality to marry you." From then on I knew his fondest hope was that I would marry her one day.

After Graham and I had been dating awhile, Mama invited her to a restaurant for lunch. That night as I was dressing to go out with another young lady, Mama said, "Son, Graham is the most beautiful person inside the body of a gorgeous woman I ever saw."

That is the first time my mother ever indicated approval of a girl I went out with. Before, she would always say, "Son, I hope you're not getting serious about that girl. You'd better watch out. She's out to get you."

"Is that bad, Mama?"

"All right, you asked my opinion, I think so."

"Why?"

"Because you are too good a person for her."

My father's attitude about girlfriends I was serious about was, "Boy, she likes men. What have you been up to, Son? Stopping by the side of the road again?"

With Graham, he said, "Son, you be careful with Graham. Don't go pulling any stunts with her."

As to marriage, he had told me numerous times, "If you get married before you finish law school, I'll cut you off financially." One day, however, he said to me, "Son, if Graham decides to have you before you get out of law school, I'll still help you financially. As a matter of fact, I'll even send a little extra." For a minute I got angry, but then I said to myself, Why should you get upset just because his taste coincides with yours?

I realized my mother and father knew more than I did about what would last and what would not. Nevertheless, their encouragement slowed me down. Whenever I spoke to another woman, Mama would say, "You getting along all right with Graham?"

I would say, "You trying to force me into something?"

"Not a bit—just trying to make you know your own heart."

"You're crowding me," I would say.

"I know you. Just because Daddy and I like Graham, you're being extra careful. You don't want us dictating to you."

"Maybe," I said.

When I finally asked Graham to marry me, and she agreed, my parents were overjoyed. Just how much Graham meant to Daddy I discovered when he told me near the end of his life: "You know, Son, I shouldn't say it. I don't mean to imply that I am the Lord or that you are Jesus, but when I think about you I always feel like that saying of the Lord about Jesus in the Bible: 'This is my son in whom I am well pleased.' But if you hadn't married Graham and had her help, I don't know if I would feel that way."

And then, lying on his deathbed just after she left his presence for the last time, he said, "That Graham is pretty and just a wonderful person."

"Well, you deserve the credit," I said. "Some of it," he replied, "some of it. A good woman can make all the difference in a man. I'm proud I helped you and Graham get together. That's one of the best things I ever did. Don't know what might have happened to you without her."

"Anyhow, Daddy," I said, "thanks."

More
to Learn

In September of 1946, right after I had undergone my intensive training with Daddy, I entered Yale Law School. Just before I left for New Haven, Justice Stanley Reed called me into his office and said, "Hugo, if you make the *Yale Law Journal,* I want you to become my clerk on graduation. I don't know how I can stand being brainwashed by your daddy from my own office in addition to the job he always does on me from his own office, but I'll try to withstand it somehow."

I had never seen students work with such dedication as everyone did in our class. When we were not studying, we were discussing the subjects in bull sessions. Because of Daddy's tutelage, as well as the bull sessions and working like a slave, I managed to finish well within the upper third of my class when the first grades came out and thereby qualified to compete for the *Yale Law Journal.*

For the next two years Graham and I, who were married by then, existed on the fifty dollars a month my father sent us, the little bit Graham made as a researcher for Yale

University, and love. As I settled into a routine of hard work my performance improved. Eventually I became an editor of the *Yale Law Journal*—although not one of its luminaries. My grades also improved, not only because of my studying but also because the number one man in the class, along with his wife, lived in the same house with me and Graham, which gave me access to his notes and the privilege of a continuing, very argumentative dialogue about the various subjects we were studying. Although miserable from the point of view of leisure, these were intellectually stimulating days.

In my third year, I was elected president of the Yale Law School Student Association. This threw me into close contact with the finest teacher I ever encountered in any school—Wesley A. Sturges, dean of the Yale Law School. In the classroom he made the dullest subject, Credit Transactions, come alive with his personality and illuminating insights. As dean, he really made use of the president of the Student Association, whoever he or she might be. For example, when some members of the faculty wanted to propose curriculum changes which other faculty members hotly opposed, he made them debate it before the students and forced me to preside. "I make you do all the dean's dirty work, Black," he would say to me.

Towards the end of the year, Dean Sturges came to me and said, "Hugo, I don't think you will be able to stand all the rottenness on the outside any better than I could. I think you can become a great teacher. I would like to propose you for a teaching fellowship next year with a view to moving you into the faculty."

I have never been more flattered before or since, but I

told him, "Dean, there are a lot of boys in my class who either have better minds or are further along than I am right now. I don't know which yet, and maybe I never will, but I just don't feel I'm ready yet." Despite his protests, I insisted that I was not sure I would like to teach. "I have other things in mind."

Unfortunately, when I graduated, I could not serve as Justice Reed's law clerk. Between the time he made his promise to me and my graduation, Congress had tightened up the nepotism statutes on federal judges. Investigation had revealed that there existed a federal court in Kentucky where every employee from the janitor on through the clerk of the court was either a father, mother, wife, brother, sister, son, daughter, aunt or uncle of the local federal judge. So Congress provided that no person above the degree of consanguinity of first cousin with a federal judge could serve in any capacity with the court on which he sat.

Disappointed that I wouldn't be able to serve as a law clerk, I made up my mind to go to Alabama to take the bar exam. Before I left, Daddy called me into his study and said, "Son, I am proud of you. Nothing can stop you now. You are on your way. Of course, I'm not going to stop bothering you. I got some reading I want you to do just as soon as you finish the bar exam. I'm looking for good copies of Aristotle's *Rhetoric*, Cicero's *Orator*, and Tacitus' *Dialogus*. Then I want to move you into Aristotle's *Poetics* and *Topics*."

When I returned from Alabama to Washington in the summer of 1949 to await the results of the bar examination, I discovered Daddy was serious about his intentions of working with me. This time we concentrated on writing and speaking as clearly as possible.

Ten years before, when he had taken his seat on the Supreme Court, my father had resolved to master the art of writing in such a way as to establish maximum communication with the largest number of people. He attacked the problem with typical enthusiasm and energy, and, as always in matters of learning, he started with the fundamentals. He began by reading articles in educational journals and then talked to writers to discover which grammar and style books were the best. In his fifties he was practicing exercises in the grammar books, memorizing the rules in them, even to the point of devising mnemonics, until he could render an idea as simply and clearly as possible.

He wrote most of his opinions with a pencil on a yellow legal pad. "If you dictate," he said, "it's so easy to let loose too many words. Talking is the easiest thing in the world. But when you got to write it yourself, your hand and arm muscles make you practice economy with your words." He could not rest until he had finished an opinion, and I have seen him do as many as six drafts before he had one ready to circulate. He searched in his mind for the precise word, often using a thesaurus or his old *Webster's Second Unabridged* to find it, and he would always select a one-syllable over a two-syllable word.

In writing his opinions he stayed away from metaphor and simile as much as possible. Once I tried to get him to use them more: "They come easy to you, Daddy, you're good at them, and they can sometimes add beauty and understanding." He replied, "They cover too many things for the kind of precision I'm looking for and it's not worth the effort to find ones that don't sound artificial."

Until I had proved myself in court and with briefs which he could commend, he never asked me for any kind of a comment on his work except one. When I had finished reading an opinion he would say, "What does it mean to you?" I would tell him, and if my understanding was what he had intended, he would say, "Good. If you can understand it that well, anybody can." A few years later, after I had passed the bar, he slipped into a Birmingham courtroom to watch me. I was taking some hard swats from the other side, whose case was bad. They abused my intelligence, my honor, my looks, my personality—everything to keep me from talking about the merits, but through all this confusion I managed to point out the merits. Afterwards he said proudly, almost half laughing, "Son, you've got a hide like a rhinoceros in the courtroom. Where did you develop that?"

I said, "I don't know, Daddy." But I thought to myself, It isn't too hard to take stuff from people you don't care about when you have had to read your hero's stuff to test out whether 'anybody' (interpret this as 'any fool') can understand it. But, of course, I never acknowledged the hurt. I always took it easy with him because he never developed a hide tough enough for me to criticize him on the direct and indirect personal basis he used with me.

In both speaking and writing, he hated artificiality. Once when he had finally gotten an opinion right after five drafts he said to me, "Man, isn't it a pity you've got to work so hard to make a piece of writing seem natural. You can bet every time you see a piece of writing that flows along naturally and easily, the author really put some hours into it." Believing everything should relate to a theme, he was careful not to qualify everything he said.

"That cuts out the muscle. If it has to be qualified, leave it out."

He emphasized over and over: "In speaking, you've got to be natural. Posing, artificial gestures, Sunday pronunciations, trying to appear important and above your audience, elocution school stuff—that's what ruins a speaker. You think I'm good on the platform, Son. Well, if there's any truth to that it's just because I stay away from all that phony stuff and try to keep loose and natural." He also said, "Give the audience some fun. Play some. Entertain even if you have to act a little bit.

"Son, don't apologize for being fiery," he said to me one day. "Fella told me my son was too fiery in his presentation. I told him, 'That's because I taught him that way.' Don't let them make you one of these New England Harvard 'stators' and elite complimenters or other quiet, prissy, one-tone 'stators'—keep doing just like you are. The real effective New England Harvard speaker has got fire just like we have. Look at Felix [Frankfurter]—he speaks with real fire and enthusiasm. And look what old, unemotional Aristotle has to say about it in *Rhetoric* or *Poetics*. Nothing wrong with using emotion for persuasion."

He taught me how to read out loud naturally with "genuine, sincere feeling. There is no reason a fella should not be able to read his stuff and hold interest. He does not have to drudge along." Once a trial judge forbade me to read testimony because I employed techniques Daddy taught me for reading with feeling. "Mr. Black," said the judge, "you might as well be making your final argument." When I told my father about this incident he said, "Well, if the testimony lines up that way, there's nothing wrong with that. That's just what the facts add up to—a large plus for your side. You couldn't do that with bad stuff."

So magnetic was his platform presence that reading from a text he could hold the attention of an audience. But he much preferred to speak without notes. "If you write a speech out, you might accidentally memorize it, and that would be bad. A fella memorizes his speeches usually ends up pontificating, and that's what I don't want to do. They come out more natural if you plan them in your head."

His public rhetoric, spoken or written, developed into a model of correctness and simple refinement. Yet at home I have heard him say "yee" for "you," or "stinjer" for "stingy." But his public speech never regressed even in his very last days. If anything, it continued to improve. I remember the Pentagon Papers opinion where he proclaimed, "In the First Amendment the Founding Fathers gave the free press the protection it must have to fill its essential role in our democracy. The press was to serve the governed, not the governors." I remember a particularly moving speech of his to the judges of his circuit, where he told them that the sun was about to set for him and he impressed on their minds that his message of "Try to be good" came from one freed from worldly cares.

Around the house, he put special demands on his own language as well as that of the rest of the family. He insisted on gentle words, and I never heard him utter even the mildest curse word in the fifty years I spent around him. He could not even bring himself to say "Hell." He would say this fellow was a "nut" or that fellow was a "fool," or even once a "Uriah Heep," but he never went further than that except when he told a story and quoted somebody else. The sole exception was when he called a man he convicted of bribing a revenue agent a crook. But he always kept his epithets low-key, and despite his reputation as a man who told it like it is, in many respects he was a master of the understatement.

Around 1892 the family of William La Fayette Black posed for this portrait on the porch of their home in Ashland, Alabama. Left to right: Orlando, Robert Lee, William La Fayette Black, Hugo, Martha Black, Daisy, Ora, Vernon, and Pelham. Courtesy of Birmingham News.

Hugo Black, Sr., as a young man.

LEFT: *During his bachelor days,*
my father enjoyed vacations on the Florida coast.
RIGHT: *Hugo Black, Sr., during World War I.*

State of Alabama,}   In the County Court of Clay, Equity Division,
Clay County.   }   Spring Term, 1906.

IN RE APPLICATION OF HUGO LAFAYETTE BLACK, FOR LICENSE TO PRACTICE AS AN
ATTORNEY AT LAW IN ALL THE COURTS OF THE STATE OF ALABAMA.

It appearing to the Court that Hugo Lafayette Black has this day filed
his application in writing to be admitted to practice as an attorney and
Counsellor at law in all the Courts of the State of Alabama, and it appearing that he is of the age of twenty years, with disabilities of non-
age removed, and is a resident of said County and State, and the Court
having made due inquiry into his moral character, and finding the same to
be good; and said Hugo Lafayette Black, having exhibited with his petition
a diploma from the University of Alabama, conferring on him the degree of
Bachelor of Laws, and the said Hugo Lafayette Black, having taken the oath
as required by section eight of Acts of Alabama, approved February, 18,
1897, Code of Alabama, 1896, p. 257, now, it is therefore considered, ordered , adjudged and decreed by the Court that Hugo Lafayette Black be permitted to practice as an attorney at law and solicitor in Chancery in all
the Courts of the State of Alabama, and the Registers certified copy of
this decree shall be his license to practice as such, which, when presented
to any Court of law or equity in the State of Alabama, shall be conclusive
evidence of his admission.
Done in Term Time at Ashland, Alabama, this the 4 day of June, 1906.

                                    W.J. Pearce
                                    Judge of the County Court of Clay.

State of Alabama,} I, Dora A. Speer, Register of the Equity Division of
Clay County.   } the County Court of Clay, hereby certify that the fore-
going contains a true and correct copy of the decree rendered by the Hon.
W.J.Pearce, Judge, Equity Division,of the County Court of Clay, on the 4
day of June, 1906, upon application of Hugo Lafayette Black for license to
practice as an Attorney at law and Solicitor in Chancery in all the Courts
of the State of Alabama. Given under my hand and seal of office on this
the 4 day of June, 1906.

                                    _____
                                            Register.

My mother, Josephine, with Sterling and myself.
Mother is pregnant with Jo-Jo.

LEFT: *Hugo campaigns in a small Alabama town.*
RIGHT: *My father and I enjoy a little sunshine.*

The "brethren" posed for this on April 17, 1939.
Top row, left to right:
Felix Frankfurter, Hugo Black, Stanley Reed, William O. Douglas.
Bottom row, left to right: Harlan Stone, J. C. McReynolds,
Charles Evans Hughes, Pierce Butler, Owen Roberts.
Courtesy of the Supreme Court.

Hugo in his office at the Supreme Court.

Economic
Radical

During the period while I was waiting to hear the results of the bar exam, I had the chance to learn more about my father's economic beliefs. Hugo was a timeless economic radical, in the sense that his radicalism was not to be found in any program yet formulated by a political party or an economic school. What he once said of Vernon Louis Parrington could apply equally well to his own beliefs: "The fella was idealistic in a way. He saw a future richer in values, much more sensible and humane than anything in the past. He was full of worldly wisdom, wise to the ways of man, very suspicious of power. But you can't say he's a communist or socialist or pin any other label on him. He's just looking for a world a little more equal in the distribution of favors and not afraid of who he hits to accomplish his aims."

"People have never proved themselves worthy of unlimited control over others," my father said to me over and over, "No special group of men has ever had that kind of power without doing wrong to the people subject to it." Then one day he added with a laugh, "Why, Son, perfect as I am, I am not sure that even I should have control without some chains."

"Daddy, I'll say amen to that. Who knows better than I?"

His smile changed to a frown. "I don't know what you mean."

I let it pass.

"Power tends to shrink into the hands of fewer and fewer people, Son. All government of the few is vicious. People don't get more honest as they get richer, they get worse. They get shadier, they get more arrogant, they feel above the law. The age-old problem is the redistribution of wealth—not just putting it into new hands, but spreading it out. You can never get the job done. As fast as you spread it, it reaccumulates just as fast, because men just aren't created equal. A few are stronger than the rest, and even meaner and more vicious when they get the power to lord it over the other fella."

"Wait a minute," I said. "Haven't you just admitted by what you said that there is a natural aristocrat, that some people are better than others? Why shouldn't they govern?"

"Son, I said they excelled in qualities of strength—self-discipline, good personal habits, personal skills—stuff that makes one man more valuable than another. I didn't say these folks could tolerate power any better. If anything, they have a worse tolerance for it."

"Something in your philosophy that bothers me has just come out again," I said. "You're sort of an aristocrat yourself. Let me go upstairs." I went to my room on the third floor and got him a letter he wrote me when it became clear that I had to remain an enlisted man in the army because of my asthma.

"On your being an enlisted man," I read, "your association will be with people who have not, in the main, had the educational opportunities of those who go to the officers' candidate schools. Many of the enlisted men do not exercise the self-restraint that officers and prospective officers are compelled to exercise. Consequently, you will find yourself with men who are sometimes reckless and daring far beyond those who have the extra responsibility of serving as leaders. This is not to say that the enlisted men are not the equals in character of any other group of people. It is said, however, with the hope of admonishing you, that temptations to deviate from established standards of sobriety and order may be greater for you in your present situation than ever before in your life."

He answered me right back: "Those differences do exist, sure. Something else, too, you've got to recognize, that people are easily deceived and turned aside from their purpose. They will be responsible if they go from their living rooms to the polls and, probably, irresponsible if they go from a mob meeting on the streets to the polls. But nevertheless, the people—except in a mob—are honest and well-meaning. They are a whole lot less likely to be mean and vicious and unjust than a privileged few of them.

"Since you brought up that letter I wrote to you in the Army, why don't you go get that other letter I wrote you when you were coming home on furlough?"

After going back upstairs, I returned to the study and sat down and read it aloud: "Enclosed I am sending you a check for $65.00. We shall be delighted to have you.

"I think I should tell you, however, that I am disappointed that you have not been able to learn in such a way that you can get along from month to month and save something for special occasions. One illustration will tell you why I have this feeling:

"I know a man now about fifty-five years of age who up to ten years ago was an outstanding liberal in his thought. He had the same gifts you have for drawing graphic word pictures. During the entire time I knew him pretty well, he was always hard-up, within one to five days of pay day. For about ten years now, he has been the paid representative of special interests whose activities he had always detested—he became a slave to them because he was first a slave to his immediate desires. He is a tragic representative of a large group of people who live in each generation who, though they have brilliant minds, finally become the paid employees of men with stodgy minds, fat stomachs and long cigars."

Putting down the letter, I commented, "Do I understand you to say, then, that the better sort of people are least likely to do right?"

"That's exactly what I'm saying—that's what Jefferson said."

"Hold on, Daddy, isn't the right whatever contributes to the natural power and splendor of our country?"

"Where did you get that stuff, Son? Doing right is whatever contributes the greatest good for the greatest number—that's all there is to it."

"Maybe that was true once," I replied, "when the farm was the economic unit. But technology has moved us from a simple to a complex economic system. Instead of deals between families on a farm, we have deals between one large institution and another. Don't you think the heads of these institutions are trying to do the best for the other people in it?"

"Bunk, Son. If they make a good deal, they'll take most of it—that's human nature. The motto of the businessman is, Do unto others that ye shall not be undone yourself. Each one of them somehow manages to believe that every other fella is a bad fella out to get him. If you say 'Be fair,' he will say 'Of course,' but just to deceive, because in his mind he will be saying 'Doesn't this nut know this is business?' After all, Alexander Hamilton, the idol of the U.S. businessman, considered men to be little more than knaves who if unrestrained would cheat the other fella as much as possible. People like that regard somebody like you or me as just a fool to be taken advantage of."

"Daddy," I said, "maybe that was true once, but I believe that maybe we are all moving towards something better."

"No, Son. People will never change. We are still governed by merchant ideals." Then he read to me from a book he had near his desk. "Listen to this, you'll think you recognize today: 'For a hundred and fifty years these merchant ideals characterized Virginia society. Speculation in land was universal, exploitation was open and shameless; the highest officials took advantage of their position to loot the public domain, resorting to divers sharp practices from tax dodging to outright theft. One gentleman added a cipher to a grant for two thousand acres and although the fraud was commonly known, so great was his influence that no one disputed his title to twenty thousand acres.' Sound familiar?"

After the first days of the Second World War, Hugo

never really felt the same about Franklin Roosevelt because it seemed to him that FDR was not continuing to look after the interests of the common man.

Daddy felt very strongly that earnings in any form—salary, wages, dividends, interest—should be limited to $25,000 per person during the war. He reasoned: "Young men are drafted. They make next to nothing and subject themselves to the risk of death or serious injury. Everything like gas, meat and the like is rationed. There is no reason these businessmen can't be limited to twenty-five thousand dollars each." But he was on the Supreme Court then, and he thought the matter was out of his jurisdiction.

Many times he brought up the matter of the federal anti-trust laws, which he felt had been purposely neglected. "I tell you, I would like to take over the anti-trust division of the Department of Justice with an unlimited budget," he told me once. "There would be no inflation then, I'll guarantee you. These fellas all sit down and fix prices and laugh about it. Some of them, of course, are beyond that. They have already merged with their buddies they fixed prices with yesterday—so they won't have to meet. They just dictate, because they control the whole matter."

"What would you do about that, Daddy?"

"Bust 'em up into little firms just like Brandeis wanted to do."

One of the biggest problems in this country, Daddy would tell me, is the tremendous difference between the highest and lowest income brackets. There has got to be a difference, of course, because of the responsibility involved, but as he would say, "it's completely nutty the way it is now. There is just no reason why a production worker in a factory should get five thousand dollars a year when the president of the firm gets five hundred thousand dollars. We got to find a solution—and soon." Along the same lines, he would also comment unfavorably every time he read an article saying the government had to grant this or that favor to the rich in order to get them to invest. "We don't need to bribe the rich to let them get richer."

In the field of taxes, there has long been a provision that each year an investor can deduct from his income tax return a part of his investment in certain properties. The deduction is for what is known as depreciation. Daddy always opposed this. "Son," he said, "this just means that the United States government sponsors this year's investors as next year's investors. Why should the taxpayer pay for the second building (if the fella uses the money for that) just because the fella had enough to build the first one?"

Inheritance was another matter that was of great concern to him, for he believed that this tends to breed an aristocracy. According to him, a widow should get enough to live as she is accustomed, but the next generation should not get anything. "Don't you count on getting anything from me," he would say. "Whatever I have to give, I will give you during my lifetime."

Although his faith in the common man might have wavered at times, he never really lost his strong belief that the people could judge, think and will act as a responsible political body if their leaders appealed to their noble side. He was quite aware of the unpleasant realities of politics, though as this note he wrote to himself reveals: "It seems difficult, however, to keep the people going forward long enough *at one time,* to produce the necessary reforms *gradu-ally*—the combined power of organized wealth and its organized propaganda never ceases to fight every honest intelligent effort to save us from the terrible abuses incident to exploitation of the many by the powerful few."

One way that Daddy kept in touch with the people was through the thousands of letters he received from all over the country. Daddy always felt they deserved a reply: "I am their servant, son. I am also one of their leaders. It is part of my duty to set them right."

Admittedly, there were many he had no chance of ever setting right, and these provided some light moments in the course of our otherwise serious conversations. I remember the man who wrote Daddy and reported that he died ten years before and that the probate judge would not issue his death certificate. This fellow wanted Daddy to force the probate judge to do his duty. Another letter we both enjoyed was from a lady who believed that her father and Daddy had walked through each other once and that Daddy wound up in her father's body. This led to all sorts of correspondence, and eventually the lady wound up writing me claiming she was my sister. Her father had been a bareback circus rider performing under the name of "The Great Diablo," and his daughter would send pictures of a barefoot "Diablo" standing on a circus pony. I used to write Daddy, enclosing her letter:

Dear Diablo:
This is your problem.

Affectionately,
Diablo, Jr.

Although Daddy always answered mail of this sort in a noncontroversial manner, I certainly didn't think it was worth his effort to answer at all. He disagreed with me, but two years after his death I was vindicated. When Justice Harry Blackmun wrote the "abortion" opinion, poor Daddy in his grave contemplating infinity was crucified about the decision—he actually received over a thousand letters of protest.

Labor
Lawyer

In the fall of 1949 I was notified that I had passed the Alabama bar exam. My father's first law clerk, Jerome "Buddy" Cooper, and his partner, Bill Mitch, invited me to join their firm in Birmingham, so in October Graham and I moved back down South. At first it was hard, especially because we couldn't afford a car, and it proved to be a real chore getting around town. Graham wanted to budget, but I had no idea how to go about it. When I tried it, everything was way out of whack. I am not sure we could have kept going had it not been for Buddy's generosity; every time he would get something extra, he would share part of it.

When we first started out, Buddy and I derived our principal income from the old CIO Southern Organizing Committee and the United Steelworkers of America. Our contact with these clients was Arthur J. Goldberg, who later became Secretary of Labor and then served on the Supreme Court. I had met him in Washington, D.C., right after law school, and he had encouraged me to go into labor law.

The CIO Southern Organizing Committee had been created to organize the industry that was rapidly leaving the unionized North in favor of the non-union Southeastern part of the United States. To put it mildly, the committee did not receive a joyous welcome when it came to a particular local community. The lawyers who formulated the strategy for industry against the committee, it has now been revealed, were the highest paid lawyers in America in those days. Frequently, the plant the committee sought to organize would be the only industry in an entire county, and the citizens believed, whether it was true or not, that when the union came in, the industry went out. In many cases the town or county had even bought bonds to build the plant in order to attract the capital. It is not surprising then that when the organizer came to town, he often found himself in jail, and when the trumped-up charge was finally brought against him, he would be taken before a local judge just licking his chops to get at the organizer and put him away "until this union stuff calmed down."

Buddy's and my job was to free the organizer. When we entered town to do our work, sometimes we had company in the form of shadows, and if we tried to hire local lawyers to help, they often would be "too busy to take on anything else—at any price."

If the organizers succeeded in getting an election ordered by the National Labor Relations Board, the company would usually commit every unfair labor practice ever heard of and invent some new ones. Long months of NLRB litigation would follow.

Whenever the committee won the election and got a certification, let us say, for the Textile Workers Union of

America, a long strike for recognition of the union by the company was sure to follow with injunction suits, contempt and criminal cases and the like. Sometimes even the Textile Workers Union lawyers got thrown in jail with the strikers, and Buddy and I had to secure their release. We would be involved in both judge and jury trials all over North Carolina, South Carolina, Tennessee, Georgia, Alabama, Mississippi, Florida, Louisiana, and sometimes Texas. Although we frequently appeared before judges whose eyes flashed hatred, there would always be friendly faces in the jury box even in very hostile territory.

As often as not we would win our case, because the company lawyers either had been careless in their arrogance or had just hoped no one would call their bluff. At worst, our clients would have their money tied up for a while in appeal bonds while our appeals pended, because we could usually settle out of court cheaply when the conflict had ceased and feeling subsided. The trick was to always have some place handy to retreat to while the heat was on.

Arthur Goldberg gave us tremendous support in those difficult days. "Labor has too frequently been represented by hacks," he once said. "I mean to bring excellence into the representation of labor unions, and you fellows are key men in that program." Occasionally, he would want to know, "Is any lawyer your age in town making more money than you?" And if there was, he saw to it that we caught up immediately. He knew that we had to travel more than we liked, and he insisted we travel first-class "so that you can at least be comfortable doing what you don't want to do." He counseled us wisely, but did not override us if we felt strongly otherwise.

For any of his clients, such as the United Steelworkers, Buddy and I knocked ourselves out. We participated in critical labor negotiations, tried to wind down wildcat strikes without offending the local union people, settled disputes between blacks and whites, appeared before congressional committees and committees of state legislatures, consulted with governors, settled disputes between unions themselves, tried landmark cases in the lower courts and made the record upon which Arthur later argued in the Supreme Court (my father abstaining), and handled all the most important labor trials in the Southeast.

Along with Bill Mitch, our other partner, Buddy and I were also involved in silicosis suits for miners, cases involving workmen's compensation, injunction and contempt, as well as labor criminal cases in the police court and the circuit court, arbitration cases, and Fair Labor Standards Act and National Labor Relations Board cases. During this time Buddy and I represented many unpopular causes, such as the black firemen and switchmen who had been ousted from their jobs by the union of white firemen and the railroad. We were able to put them back on their jobs with back pay.

When Arthur left his post and became Secretary of Labor, he left a gap that has never been filled and, perhaps, never will be again. With his departure, my taste for labor law began to sour, and I began to think about Daddy's advice to me when I first moved to Alabama. "You've got to avoid becoming indebted to anyone else financially or otherwise and sacrificing any of your integrity of decision. You can't let any one client or clients become your sole source of income."

During the time when my professional career was gradually being established, I was also beginning to learn what it meant to be a father. Hugo Black III was born in 1953, Elizabeth Graham Black in 1956, and Margaret Hartley Black in 1957.

When Daddy would visit me and Graham during this period, he would often become concerned about the number of offenses involving violence that I was defending, and the arguments I used in behalf of my clients in those cases. "Son," he would say, "I don't want you to forget what I've been teaching you all your life about law and order and the need to obey the law." Although this principle of obedience to the law, applied in his Supreme Court opinions, eroded his reputation for liberalism and enhanced his reputation for conservatism, it was something he stuck by all his life. Before my father entered the Senate I remember an incident involving a policeman he knew. Daddy was illegally parked, but the policeman recognized him and wanted to tear up the ticket. "Ralph," he told the policeman, after insisting that he be given the ticket, "let this be a lesson. Make *no* exceptions. That's what I thought I taught you fellas. Don't forget again."

Sometimes when we came to a red light in a deserted section of the countryside he would stop. "Daddy," I'd say, "nobody's coming. There aren't any cops around. Let's go."

"Son, you've got to obey the law automatically, no matter what the chance of getting caught there is." Of course, he was not perfect. I would catch him going over the speed limit occasionally or passing in a no-passing zone. But in Washington, he never took advantage of the sort of diplomatic immunity congressmen enjoyed, and in fact he never thought it was right that senators and diplomats were "above" all the traffic laws.

Once in Birmingham when Daddy brought up the issue of obeying the law, I reminded him that even Jefferson believed you had the right to disobey an unjust law and the right to rebel against an oppressive government.

"Well, they are two different things," he replied. "As to the rebellion, the old saying tells it all, 'If you shoot at the king, you better kill him.' As to your duty to obey an unjust law, nobody has got a right to pick and choose between the laws on their own notions of right and wrong or natural law or such stuff. You've just got to obey the law—period."

"What about Thoreau? He said you've got a duty of civil disobedience, a duty to disobey an unjust law."

"Yeah, Son, but he also meant you would pay the price for disobeying it. The publicity about your punishment might get the thing repealed, but Thoreau would have been furious at these nuts who claim they've got the right to spit on any law, to make others do what they want and expect to get away with it."

Some of my labor union clients caused Daddy to get very agitated. "You always seem to represent these nuts who beat people in the head with a ball bat in the name of some cause."

"Well, Daddy," I said, "they've got a right to representation."

"But I don't want you to think they got a right to bully people with physical violence to accomplish what they think is the right. It isn't moral to beat people in the head to bring about even something that's good for everybody. You just can't do that kind of stuff and have a society."

"It isn't as bad as these fat cats who cheat people out of everything they have with lies and fraud—"

"Son, the law doesn't get to fraud until it controls violence."

"Daddy," I said, "how can you advocate obeying a law that you really believe is evil?"

"Son, we can't have a society unless you can count on most people automatically obeying the law—no matter how bad it is. The answer to bad laws is to elect people like me and other good men to put good laws in place of the bad. If you do it any other way, it's anarchy. And any government is better than anarchy."

In his business dealings my father was very scrupulous about practicing what he preached. A few years before he went into the Senate he became one of the owners of a bank, a move he later regretted since he admitted he didn't know anything about banking. When the Depression came, the depositors panicked; there was a run on the bank and it failed. Many of the depositors and creditors remained unpaid out of the remaining assets, but then my father and one other organizer paid them all off in full, even though the other owners simply had nothing and could not pay their pro rata shares. Selling his assets at depression prices depleted the entire little fortune Daddy had accumulated as a lawyer.

Some enemies might say that he paid because he was a senator, and if he had not, he could not have continued in office. I do not believe this for one minute. If he had not paid everyone back, he would not have destroyed the expectations of a single depositor or creditor of the time. They expected to lose, and they expected nothing beyond the call of duty from a politician still in power. Hugo did it because of his strong sense of law and order. "If everybody won't do what the other fella and I did," he told me, "then the system just won't work."

Reading

While I was practicing law in Birmingham, Daddy frequently observed, "You ought to be able to get a lot of helpful reading in, son, with all this traveling around on planes and staying away from home in hotels." To his dying day, Daddy strongly believed in reading, and enthusiastically consumed books in which he would not only underline passages but also write comments in the margins, and then index his notes in the back. He devoured everything written about the Founding Fathers. A skilled writer could take my father's copy of a tract written by James Madison or Thomas Jefferson, for example, and from the text and the notes jotted in the margin by my father, render a spirited conversation between the two about contemporary constitutional problems.

In the main, he avoided novels, poetry, plays, artistic criticism, or any such works of the imagination. The only exceptions were *Remembrance Rock* by Carl Sandburg, the plays of Aeschylus, Sophocles and Shakespeare, and the poems of Milton and Goldsmith, all of which he regarded as instructive, sound examples of unchanging human nature. What he loved most were books about Greek, Roman, British, American or French history and essays on politics, economics and law. Gibbon's *The Rise and Fall of the Roman Empire*, Toynbee's unabridged *Study of History*, Thucydides' *Peloponnesian War*, and Beveridge's *Life of John Marshall* were studied and annotated by him. He also read anything he could find on Thomas Jefferson and Andrew Johnson, both of whom he considered great men.

According to my father, Dostoevsky, Kirkegaard, Mann, Hemingway and Joyce were worthless, and Melville, Proust, Kafka and Camus were bores, whose mission, if any, seemed to be to corrupt humanity. As far as surrealism went, he thought the "nuts" who created it should count their blessings that they were free and had not been confined in an asylum. The works of Freud that "invented this fool unconscious" that these "fool surrealists" used to "rationalize nonsense" on a canvas or a page were to him just plain fraudulent pretense. I remember one day when he was sitting at home reading a book on psychiatry. This was after my sister Jo-Jo had graduated from Swarthmore and was being psychoanalyzed to fulfill a requirement for becoming a psychiatric social worker. Suddenly he put down the book and cried out, "Good Lord. This is the biggest fool statement I ever saw anywhere. This nut advises you to lose your temper, blow off steam. He says controlling your temper is what causes psychiatric distress. Well, tell me now, who is going to like some nut who goes around indulging his temper and hollering and screaming bad things? When everybody starts avoiding this poor nut that the psychiatrist has set off in temper tantrums, he is really gonna be in distress."

After he was on the Court, he selected his reading strictly on the basis of whether it would help him in his job one way or another. Although a well-rounded intellectual might say his reading list was spotty, he did read and remember an incredible number of books. Edith Hamilton's *The Greek Way* was a favorite, as well as Parrington's *Main Currents in American Thought,* which he thought reflected the conflict between the "plain people" and those who exploited them. "This really is the struggle that's been going on since the beginning of history," he would say.

Hugo loved Plutarch, as might be expected of a public man who considered the poor, the weak and the powerless his personal responsibility. Daddy's favorite biography in Plutarch's *Lives* was that of Tiberius and Gaius Gracchus, who were murdered after espousing the cause of the helpless poor. He was also intrigued by Plutarch's *Essays,* and was always quick to recommend "Contentment" to anyone who was moaning and unhappy and yet had three fine meals a day, fine clothes and a fine house.

Whatever Daddy could find about Marcus Aurelius, the Philosopher King, he would devour. Nothing ever subverted his faith in democracy except what he concluded by reading about Marcus Aurelius. "Son," he said, "if all absolute rulers acted like Marcus Aurelius we wouldn't need democracy. The fella decrees good without debate, without some nut to talk him into something bad. But just look at his successors, then you know why we've got to have democracy."

Nobody ever got more out of the Harvard Classics than my father did. He read everything in them he thought might do him some good. Once in the Senate, shortly after a debate started between himself and Senator Kenneth McKellar of Tennessee, Hugo went to the Congressional Library for Volume 27 of the Harvard Classics. Senator McKellar had conceded that Daddy's reform measure had merit, but he insisted that the bill was before its time. After returning to the Senate floor, Hugo got him to yield to a question. "Senator, are you making 'The Procrastinator's Argument'?"

"And what is that, Senator?"

"I will send it to you, Senator."

Hugo sent to Senator McKellar the book he had just got from the library opened to an essay entitled "Fallacies of an Anti-Reformer": "Wait a little. This is not the time. This is the common argument of men, who, being in reality hostile to a measure, are ashamed or afraid of appearing to be so."

Senator McKellar read it; then he double-talked for a couple of minutes and sat down. "Hugo, where'd you find this damned thing?" he asked later.

"I own Harvard Classics," Daddy replied. "They are full of stuff like that, Senator."

"How about my side?" Senator McKellar asked.

"It's there, Senator."

"Where?"

"Find it yourself," Daddy replied with a smile.

What Daddy read in his lifetime fills two study rooms, and many of his books with underlinings and marginal notes have now been put on display in the United States Supreme Court Building. If he had known this was to happen, he would probably have had me burn his books, because he underlined and commented not only on what he agreed with, but also on what he took issue with or thought silly. Any attempt to interpret his notes and underlinings must be done with extreme caution. But as long as these books are studied with this in mind, I believe they can serve scholars and historians well.

619 South Lee Street

 formula

While my father was in the Senate we owned a two-story, white shingled house in Wesley Heights that had appreciated substantially in value. But since we had to rent it out whenever Congress adjourned, my father decided it might be simpler to rent the house out all year around. Even though my mother wanted to own a house, we went through a period of renting houses for ourselves when Congress was in session. Mama loved the area around Seminary Hill in Alexandria, Virginia, up near the Virginia Episcopal Seminary. That is where her sister and brother-in-law, Virginia and Cliff Durr, lived. But all the while Mama had her eye on a lot on Seminary Hill, and she even commissioned an architect to sketch the house of her dreams. When Daddy heard of this, he insisted it would be too expensive, so for the time being mother had to be content with other people's houses.

Shortly after my father was appointed to the Supreme Court, Mama tried a new tack. While visiting the old sections of Alexandria, she found what was known as the

Snowden Home, an example of Georgian architecture, part of which had been built in 1740. It was a great house all right, but badly in need of renovation. After my father took a look at it, the first thing he said to her was, "It's not only that it is in such bad shape, but look at that house next to it. It's horrible. And look at the lot the house you want is on. Good Lord, darling, it runs right out to the open slum."

My mother was not easily discouraged, though, and insisted there was a way to make this into a nice home. Eventually, she and my father decided that it would be possible to buy the shabby-looking house next door and tear it down, and then build a wall around the property. Instead of borrowing money, they would simply swap the house in Wesley Heights for this place.

The next thing we knew, Daddy had taken over. A wrecking crew arrived and was soon busy tearing down the old house next door. Trucks began dumping bricks out in piles at intervals along the boundary for the new Justice Black Compound. Carpenters, brick masons, electricians and plumbers all went to work bringing the house up to date. Then to our surprise Daddy announced that he had decided to build a tennis court, and almost immediately he began bringing home all sorts of books on how to construct them. There were endless discussions with everybody about what would be the right height for a fence that would stop all but the wildest mis-hits, and how much of this should be of brick and how much of anchor fence. He not only studied to see what type of court would do the least damage to the players' legs, but he also spent hours considering the effect of the sun on the players. When the actual construction began, he supervised every step of the way; and during one morning inspection he even made the workers add more gravel to the pit that would be the foundation of the clay court.

When all of this activity was finished, we had a real showplace with the tennis court as the central attraction. Out in the yard, my father had planted rhododendrons from North Carolina, scuppernong grapes (a variety of muscadine) from Clay County, Alabama, and fig, peach, pear and apple trees. A tree surgeon was hired to look after the existing cherry, buckeye and English walnut trees and English boxwoods on the grounds. Hugo also put in a vegetable garden where the old house used to stand, and each spring corn, okra, beans and peas were planted for the summer. He always liked to have berries around too—one season it would be blueberries, the next blackberries, and the next raspberries.

The yard and the tennis court kept him close to home and provided him with new concerns. Spencer Campbell —who had worked for our family for over forty years in various capacities, such as cook, chauffeur, butler, and Daddy's court messenger, as well as being a bosom companion to Sterling and myself—and Daddy would work together on all the problems that arose, both of them watering and spraying and mowing to keep everything in shape.

Daddy always worried about his trees and plants being victimized by "the law of the jungle." There was a running battle with the Japanese beetles in his rose garden and, unlike Grandpa Foster, he never was able to defeat them. Tent caterpillars regularly camped out in his trees and banqueted on the leaves. So far as I know, he and Spencer knew only one way to fight back. They would pull up a step ladder and station it under the tree, then light a kerosene-soaked rag tied to the end of a long pole and burn the caterpillars' tent. This treatment would get the tent all right, but sometimes the caterpillars would drop down onto Daddy. When that happened, he'd drop the pole and make a real fuss, batting his hands all about and yelling for help.

The birds also gave Spencer and him a very difficult time. One large buckeye tree in the front yard branched over a prime parking area in front of our house, but Daddy forbade any of us to park there. "Those birds will splat the top of the car every time you park there, Son, and you can't get that stuff off. Deadly, too, eats right through the paint in minutes and that's one hundred dollars." The birds also pecked at his cherries and grapes. Short of shooing them away, he and Spencer could not find a way to get rid of them—until they hit upon the idea of using the "silver disks." These were pieces of aluminum foil suspended from the tree stems or vines which would reflect the sun's rays and supposedly scare off the birds. No doubt they helped to some degree, but the "musket irons" (as Daddy called the muscadines) I picked to eat would likely as not have holes pecked in them.

The squirrels were another of his personal enemies. They came in what we called squirrel herds in the fall, chattering and sunning about happily until they had finished off his English walnuts for the season. Daddy was constantly thinking up ways to "whip this squirrel problem." Finally, he found out about a squirrel trap, and began to catch a few of them. He would usually get Spencer to take the animal off down the Mt. Vernon Highway somewhere and turn it loose, since he just did not have it in him to kill one.

Daddy and Spencer not only had the yard to tend, but

also had to care for the tennis court. To keep the court in the perfect condition he liked took a lot of work. Whenever I was visiting, I used to help him prepare the court in the evening for an early morning game. First we would sprinkle it, then roll it and finally line it—a laborious process. While sometimes I was annoyed by his constant supervision ("Turn the nozzle, Son, you're sprinkling too heavy"), we were able to have some interesting conversation about the Court as well as talk over family matters.

Promptly at seven the next morning he would be ready to use the freshly tended court. We would practice serves and different strokes, and at noon we would pause for a cold beer and a nap. Then we'd be back on the court until the setting sun shining in our eyes made it impossible to do anything but get the court ready for the next day. Once after a strenuous day of tennis, while we were all sitting out on the terrace listening to the chirping of the crickets, Daddy said, "Man, who needs any more than this?"

Josephine

〰️

I think one reason my parents' marriage worked was that their personalities complemented each other so well. Daddy had a sixth sense about how the "average man" thought and felt, and he truly cared about humanity, but he shied away from most individuals and definitely was not extraordinarily sensitive to what made a particular individual tick. Mama, on the other hand, loved and understood individual people, whoever they were and no matter how different they were. She used to laugh and say, "I have a radar that tells me what is going on inside their minds." And she tried to get her family to develop the same kind of perception and sympathy. "There is no need to hurt or demean people," she would say. "After seeing you they should always leave thinking more of themselves than when they came." She constantly corrected Daddy, in her very gentle way, about the feelings of persons he was dealing with. Daddy unfailingly accepted her advice about how to treat them because she never made a mistake.

Although my father could be a barrel of fun, he always felt guilty about being frivolous, and he really needed Mama to encourage him. Sometimes when she found him engrossed in work she would knock his book out of his hands and laughingly say, "Now, you think up something for us to do."

One day Mama decided to teach Daddy a lesson. Since he always insisted that no one needed more than one pair of shoes, she took his one pair and hid them. For an hour he went all over the house asking us to help him find his shoes. Finally Mama said, "If you had two pairs, you could—" Daddy caught on, and he chased her all around the house swatting her on the fanny as she said, "Stop it, you nut. Stop it. I'm not used to this exercise."

I also remember the time my mother decided Daddy should start having a drink before dinner. "You are too much of a puritan," she said. "You need to loosen up."

"I don't want to," Daddy grumbled. "I'm afraid of the stuff." But she made him do it and he began to enjoy sipping a cocktail and talking before dinner.

Daddy never had time for appreciating the natural beauty that abounds in this world, but Mama seemed to derive inner peace from it and wanted to teach her children to love nature too. Down through the years, in places like Long Beach, Mississippi; Point Clear, Alabama; the mountains in Mentone, Alabama; Washington; and wherever we went, she taught us to enjoy sunrises and sunsets, fireflies, blinking stars, clouds shaped like people's faces, rocks washed clean by pure creek water tumbling down a mountainside and the sunlight reflected through a dewdrop clinging to a blade of grass. She listened with me to the music of crickets and tree frogs in the night, to the waves, and to the unexpected quiet of snowflakes falling to the earth. We used to write bad poems about these wonders, closeting ourselves in our separate rooms, and then reading them to each other later.

After Daddy was appointed to the Court, Mama began writing short stories and poetry in earnest, working very hard on them whenever she had a spare moment. She even signed up for courses in creative writing. Because she did not want to sell just because she was Mrs. Hugo Black, she submitted her stories to magazines under pen names. But all she got was rejection slips.

At this time, my mother was exploring Far Eastern religions, extrasensory perception and transcendentalism in an attempt, as she put it, "to get in tune with the cosmos." She read Mary Baker Eddy and seriously considered Christian Science, and once she even visited a medium. But none of these things ever really fulfilled her, since they failed to give her the vision beyond the senses she was looking for.

As I said earlier, Mama had a unique capacity for inspiring a sense of self-worth in others and for calming an agitated mind. As a consequence, people who were upset came to her one after the other and poured out their souls —her father, her sister and nieces and nephews, store clerks, gas station attendants as well as the wives of senators, congressmen, Supreme Court justices and their clerks—even the wife of a future President. She listened, and invariably they left in a better state of mind.

There came a time, however, when her strength gave out and she herself became very depressed and overwhelmed with guilt feelings she could not describe. Daddy grieved, but if anything, he adored her more after her trouble began than before. He wondered if he had caused it, and searched his memory for hours on end looking for reasons for her depression. When he asked her whether he had contributed to it in any way she only said to him, "All you have done is love me with all your heart and soul—when I am not worthy of that kind of devotion. But that couldn't possibly be what it is. I just don't know what it is."

Occasionally tears came into my father's eyes because he could do nothing. "Son, we got to do something for her, I shouldn't say this to you, because I know you love me. But nothing matters to me besides her—nothing." Then some days he could only say, "I am helpless."

Whether this depression was partly a result of the physical changes of menopause combined with psychological pressures, I cannot say for sure. Or it could have been the result of a self-fulfilling prophecy—she thought she was doomed to collapse because both her father and, in the end, her mother, had suffered breakdowns. Or she might have yearned to accomplish in her own right, separate and apart from Daddy, and felt that she had not. It is also possible that a large part of her pervasive feeling of hopelessness was simply the accumulation of sadness from the hours of listening to and counseling distressed people, whose pains I am sure she shared. Mama, having no one like herself to go to, sought the help of psychiatry. But that seemed to help very little, and she continued to suffer real torture.

There was no dramatic change that marked a return to normal for her, but a step in the right direction was taken when she started to paint, for here she found a way to uniquely express herself. She had a natural gift for color, and one art critic actually compared her color sense to that of Matisse, while another said, "Her paintings have an ethereal spiritual quality." She applied herself with stern discipline, beginning with basic courses at the Corcoran Art Gallery, and spending many hours working in a studio she fixed up at our house in Alexandria.

Josephine painted under several aliases; one would not do, as she was afraid that it would be discovered that this fictitious person was in reality Mrs. Hugo Black. Before long her paintings began to win prizes, and then they began to sell. As her success as a painter continued to grow, her depression gradually faded away, and in the last year of her life, she appeared more serene than I had ever seen her.

"Son, what do you think about your mother?" Daddy said to me one day when I was home in Washington.

"Daddy, I think she has it licked."

"Oh, man, I'm glad you feel that way too. She seems so happy these days. I just don't see how she could have ever felt unworthy. I just don't see it. She is the greatest human being ever lived."

"Daddy, that may be a little strong."

His eyes flashed, and he said in a voice charged with indignation, "It is not, Son. I've watched her. What she does for these people—" And he shook his head.

A few months before she died she drew me to her and kissed me. "I have worked through this thing," she said. "I have worked through it. I have never felt such peace in all my life."

One Man's
Religion

Unlike Josephine, my father did not seem concerned about seeking a higher spiritual awareness. Although he had a profound commitment to a code of moral values, he could not whip himself up into a belief in God or the divinity of Christ, life after death, or Heaven or Hell. He passionately wanted to believe but he just could not. "Understand," he said to me once, "I cannot believe. But I can't not believe either."

When we lived in Wesley Heights in Washington, Mama enrolled us in Sunday School at the Canterbury Methodist Church, the only church within walking distance. Since we had no religious guidance at home, Sterling and I did pretty much what we pleased at Sunday School. We made wisecracks, formed a "back seat choir" by dominating the singing in our off-key voices, and challenged the teacher's statements.

We tried to get at Daddy by asking him why he didn't attend church. Although he always excused himself with something about getting ready for a speech or debate the next day, I later figured out that this was the only time he could spend with Mama without our roaming around the house.

Remembering all the stories he told me about teaching the Bible in Alabama, I asked him one day how he reconciled being such a legendary church person in Alabama and never going to church in Washington. "Son, that's easy," he replied. "All I did was teach the Bible in Alabama; those parts I selected, I taught. I didn't have to go listen to the preacher." To him the Bible wasn't a profession of faith but, rather, a book that had more lessons to give for a constructive life than any other work. In the New Testament he read the sayings attributed to Jesus himself, and he liked to read me a parable and question me on its meaning. Invariably, he thought I got it wrong. I remember once when he was asking me about the parables of equal pay for unequal work and the prodigal son.

"Daddy," I protested, "that's not just unjust, that's bad. The deserving guy gets ignored."

"Good Lord," he would say. "You of all people. No use my trying to explain. You aren't ready yet for the lesson."

"What do you mean, Daddy?" I would say, mad as a snake and ready to uncoil at him. By the time I thought I understood why he read these parables to me, he no longer did. Perhaps one of the things he wanted to make clear was that a late bloomer received blessings at least equal to those for an early bloomer.

He must have read to me a thousand times from the 13th Chapter of First Corinthians: "Charity . . . envieth not; charity vaunteth not itself, is not puffed up, . . . is not easily provoked; thinketh no evil; rejoices not in iniquity, but rejoices in the truth; Beareth all things, believeth all things, hopeth all things, endureth all things." This to him was the most important lesson in life.

Daddy enjoyed explaining religious lessons to me. "Son," he said, reading out of a book as he lay in bed at night, "Here's the central core of all religions. See if you see the similarity. Christianity: 'Do unto others as you would have them do unto you.' Now here's where Confucius was asked: 'Is there one good word that sums up the basis of all good conduct?' And Confucius replied, 'Is not reciprocity the word? What you yourself do not desire, do not put before others.' Listen to this, Mohammedanism: 'No one is a true believer until he loves for his brother what he loves for himself.' And, listen, ever hear of Shintoism? 'One should not be mindful of suffering in his own life and unmindful of suffering in the lives of others.' Now here's Taoism. 'He is fit to govern who loves all people as he loves himself.'

"Know what, Son? That Golden Rule about sums up right conduct, doesn't it? Try to live by it. Don't get discouraged if you fail, but try."

Something in the way he had read all of it was like clean, cool water in springtime rushing down a mountain to nourish the roots of a young oak. Sound crazy? Well, maybe it does, but when he talked like that he created visions like that in my head, and he was able to move me in ways no other person ever could. I'll never forget another time I was deeply affected by his words. "Son," he said, "I've had it all except being President. Looking back, only one thing counts. Try to live your life so that the people who know you best feel like putting up a tombstone over your remains that says 'Here lies a good man.' If anybody feels like doing that, who's lived close to you during your life, you have achieved what it's all about."

Although Daddy had been a courtroom lawyer and politician, professions where shady practices are hardly uncommon, he insisted that he never resorted to guile or deception to get his way. Ethical conduct, his real religion, was of paramount importance to him. Once, in testing him on his theory that the first ten amendments to the Constitution had been incorporated into the Fourteenth Amendment, I insinuated that he took this extreme position just to drag the fainthearted to the middle, where they should be. He exploded: "That's foolishness. The authors intended to incorporate those ten amendments in the thing when they drafted it. I've studied it, I know. I am not capable of that kind of guile." I believed him. It is certainly possible his incorporation theory is wrong, but it is not possible that he thought so and still espoused it. He had convinced himself of the truth of any proposition that he ever urged as a public man. Some might say he had an infinite capacity to deceive himself, but, nevertheless, whenever he was aware of any use of guile he was heartily offended. It's no wonder then that when he found me reading books such as Machiavelli's *The Prince* or Gracián's *Manual*, he tried to show me how despicable they were.

One day, to my surprise, he voiced his concern about the decline in popularity of organized religion. "This stuff's been a great foundation for doing right. Some people got to be scared into doing the right thing, some others got to be given blind hope you gonna find it better somewhere else by doing right on this earth. You pull out faith in God and these incentives to do good disappear."

"Wait a minute," I said. "Are you saying you are a bad man?"

"Aw, Son. I'm not talking about fellas like us who just do good for the sake of it, study ethics and the Bible and know in their minds you got to treat the other fella the way you want him to treat you to keep society together —it's the fella who's got to get it some other way."

"Well, Daddy, you haven't done the cause of organized religion a lot of good lately by your example."

He hung his head. "Now, Son, what do you want me to be—a hypocrite?"

"You belong in church pushing moral lessons more than anybody."

"Yeah, Son, but I couldn't do it. If I went, I'd just have to listen to some fella who loves to talk about nothing."

Although he believed that the advantages of organized religion outweighed its ill effects, he felt hostility to certain historical events involving churches and to certain church practices. Religion to him was an intensely personal thing, and he felt outrage about any church's attempt to encourage belief by compulsion. He believed that it was only natural that any church would hungrily welcome a close relationship with the state, and since the Catholic Church enjoyed the privilege of being the state church in Spain, he suspected it of aspiring to the same relationship in the United States. He could not tolerate any sign of encouraging religious faith by state aid. When he wrote his opinion holding compulsory prayer in the schools unconstitutional as an "establishment of religion" under the First Amendment and caused a storm of protest, he said to me, "Most of these people who are complaining, Son, are pure hypocrites who never pray anywhere but in public for the credit of it. Prayer ought to be a private thing, just like religion for a truly religious person."

Shock and
Bereavement

The first time I ever really understood, down to the very marrow of my bones, that my father needed someone at his side was the day Mama died—December 7, 1951. She was in her fifty-first year, he in his sixty-fourth.

When my wife, Graham, and I arrived at 619 South Lee Street from Birmingham that night, I rushed upstairs to him. I needed help, and I almost broke my neck getting up there to the study, where I was used to getting help. But this time, it was different. He was there all right, sitting in a chair behind his desk piled high with law books, and on it was a yellow pad with a half-finished opinion in his own handwriting. But the figure there looked like nothing I'd ever seen before. He just sat staring straight ahead, tears shining on his face, his teeth grinding together.

"Daddy, Daddy," I said, holding myself in. But he said nothing, did not even acknowledge my presence.

"Daddy, what happened? Tell me how it happened."

He didn't move, just said, "I don't know."

I went over to him and shook him and said again, "Tell me how it happened."

He couldn't, though. He was in a trance, and he stayed that way until I got him undressed and into bed. I don't think he slept any; I peeped in on him a couple of times, and his eyes were wide open.

That night I found out from Lizzie Mae that Mama had had a cold for a couple of days and had been sleeping in my room. My brother Sterling, who had been visiting there, left the night before. She had not been able to see him off because of her cold, and had written him a letter which was out on the dresser in the hall. Then she had gone up to go to sleep—her last sleep.

The next morning, Lizzie Mae Campbell—Spencer's beautiful sister who had worked for Daddy since 1937— checked in on Mama to see if she wanted any breakfast, but she appeared to be asleep. Lizzie Mae and Daddy decided to let her sleep.

By noon, Daddy had gotten a little worried, and he seemed to sense something was wrong. He and Lizzie Mae conferred and they decided she should go and wake Mama up. No sooner had she gotten up there than Lizzie Mae hollered for Daddy. He rushed upstairs and felt for Mama's vital signs, but found none. At this point the story is confused because no one seemed quite sure what happened. Apparently Daddy did not accept her death then. He immediately thought of heart massage and asked Dr. Paul Dickens, whom he had called, how to do it. After trying it for a while, he finally realized nothing would work and then sank into the pitiful state he was in when we arrived.

Lizzie Mae had to make arrangements with the doctor and the funeral home all on her own. My father simply could not help. He was almost, but not quite, as bad the next morning after we arrived. He took up his station at his desk and commenced to stare. The first thing he said to me was, "Son, I waited and waited because I didn't want to marry a woman who would die before me. I thought about it and thought about it."

"I know, Daddy," I said, rubbing him on the head. After we sat awhile, he added, "Son, there's no such thing as natural justice. That's the best human being ever I ran into, the best, sweetest, most thoughtful, most unselfish. She ought to be the last to die of her generation—not one of the first. Life is wrong—it's just wrong."

I mumbled, "That's right" or some other inanity. I was worried about the funeral arrangements and when I finally asked him about this, he said, "I don't care, Son, I don't care. Do what you want. What difference does it make."

"Daddy—"

"I told you, Son, I told you," he said forcefully.

Jo-Jo got in that day from Swarthmore, and she, Graham, Lizzie Mae, Sterling and Mr. Waggaman, the marshal of the Court, and I made all the funeral arrangements. Because I had heard Mama and Daddy talk about being buried together in Arlington Cemetery—she was entitled in her own right because of her service as a Navy Yeomanette, he because of his service as a captain in the Artillery —Jo-Jo, only eighteen at the time, went with me to pick out the grave site. We rejected several places until we came to one under a big oak tree, far up on the hill. Jo-Jo and I knew that this was a perfect spot for both of them. For Mama, because of its natural beauty: it was comforting to imagine her resting here on this hill, where you could witness brilliant sunrises and sunsets, a spot which on some nights would be bathed in the glow of a full moon or the more remote light of the stars. And as for my father, I was sure he would approve of it for his own resting place when his time came, since there was a good view of the national memorial of his hero Thomas Jefferson.

Although Daddy was able to greet the people who came to the funeral, he was not really my father at all. He was an automaton that we had to wind up to make him go through mechanical motions. He remained in a trancelike state of depression—no good to himself or anybody else.

I had to fly back to Birmingham for a couple of days right after the funeral. As the plane circled over National Airport, I looked over toward Arlington and saw a sight that put me in mind of her—a sunset caught in the clouds, transforming them into a gorgeous, ephemeral lake. Picking up my pen, I tried to capture on paper what I saw. I don't know exactly why I've kept what I wrote, except that I guess I hope sometime, someplace, I'd have a chance to share it with her.

When I returned to Washington a few days later, I was very worried about Daddy. In order to get him out of the house for a change of scenery, I suggested we go for a ride. He neither agreed nor disagreed, but simply allowed himself to be pushed along. When I asked if we should go to Mama's grave site, he said, "I'm not ready for that." Instead we drove out to Mount Vernon, a half-hour's drive, during which he hardly spoke at all. I felt pretty discouraged on the trip back to Alexandria. When we pulled up in front of 619 South Lee Street, I started to park the car under the big buckeye tree when he roared at me, "Good Lord, Son, how many times I got to tell you not to park the car here where the birds can do something on it. You know how that bird stuff messes up the paint. Why do you keep on doing it?"

I knew then that he would be all right and would return to normal soon. When he got back into the house, he went right back to his post in the chair behind his desk. I followed him into the study and noticed the same unfinished opinion lying there, exactly as I had seen it when I first came in from Birmingham. Casually picking up the yellow pad from the desk, I began to study it. He didn't even notice, just sat there staring straight ahead.

After a little while, I said, "I didn't know you'd been trying to work since she died."

He looked around at me. "I haven't—what makes you say that?"

I glanced down again at the page and said, "I'm sorry, Daddy, I shouldn't have disturbed you."

"Why—you look as if there's something the matter with it," he said. "Let me see it. What's wrong with it?" And he reached across and took the pad away from me.

"Well, it's the organization—and there is a conclusion wholly unjustified by the premise."

"Come over here, show me, you don't know what you're talking about. Show me." Then we took off. About four and a half hours later, he had finished the beautiful opinion he had started before she died. And he did not stop working for another twenty years.

Hugo and the
Supreme Court

I think it can be fairly said that until my father was appointed to the Supreme Court and the conservative–liberal balance changed, that institution was used by the privileged to put the underprivileged back in their place. It was still John Marshall's court, where the law of business was the law of the land, and no populistic tampering with that law by legislators was allowed. When Daddy arrived—he replaced Justice Willis Van Devanter—he determined to do all he could to make the Supreme Court and the court system which it bestrides a haven for the helpless, weak, outnumbered and non-conforming victims of prejudice that he believed the founders of our government intended courts to be. And he intended to bring this about through a living law based on the Constitution, a law that would possess elements of permanency to withstand the shifting political winds which blow one day for the superprivileged and the next for the underprivileged, even though this frequently meant passing up opportunities based on the raw power of the Court to do right as its members saw it. If liberals passed up the opportunity to use the raw power of the Court without regard to a philosophy of permanency ensured by the Constitution, Hugo believed that it would make it more difficult "for the reactionaries to do the right as they see it—the wrong as I see it—when they recapture the raw power of the Court, which they inevitably will."

Hugo detested phrases such as "natural law," "shock the judicial conscience," and "balancing," which he considered mere subterfuges for a judge who is just enforcing his own notion of the right as he sees it. Whenever someone argued by claiming that elements of permanency could not be translated into living constitutional law because the problems that come before the Court differ in every age, Hugo would reply, "Human nature doesn't change; the problems this court deals with all originate in human nature. The more things change, the more they remain the same."

My father felt that the key to transforming the Supreme Court into a sanctuary for the powerless lay in the words of the First Amendment:

> Congress shall make no law respecting an establishment of religion, or prohibiting the free exercise thereof; or abridging the freedom of speech, or of the press; or the right of the people peaceably to assemble, and to petition the Government for a redress of grievances.

Once he started talking about the First Amendment, there was no stopping him. Daddy's conviction grew with each passing year that these words mean more to the preservation of our democratic republic than any others. Before him, no Justice ever looked at the First Amendment and read "no law" to mean no law. Every other Justice had interpreted them to mean that "no law" could be passed unless there was a "clear and present danger" that the words might be translated into action, or unless the words were obscene or libelous. But for my father there were no exceptions. I have studied the amendment and it appears to me that my father's interpretation is correct, but I admit to prejudice and acknowledge that a number of constitutional scholars think it wrong. No one can say, however, that Daddy and Justice William Douglas have not, by adopting this interpretation, rendered expression freer and safer by making any compromise closer to "no law."

Daddy took a lot of ridicule for this interpretation, but it did not bother him. He chuckled whenever he told this anecdote: "Why, right after I really understood that 'no law' means no law and announced it, a certain critic of mine wrote me a letter and said that he had been wanting to express his opinion of me for a long time, but had been afraid of the libel laws. 'Now,' he said, 'I am at last free under your interpretation of the First Amendment to express my precise opinion of you. Mr. Justice, you are a sonofabitch.' " Others paraded examples of extreme libel and obscenity before him, thinking to drive him off his position, but he would reply without the slightest hesitation that the First Amendment is absolute. "It prohibits passing any law to prohibit that stuff, bad as you might think it is. The founders knew that libel and obscenity had been used as excuses to tyrannize free speech."

Some critics said that Hugo did not really mean "no

law" because by narrowing his definition of speech, press and assembly he could refuse to strike down a law which actually did abridge that right. Daddy conceded that this was theoretically possible, but that he couldn't conceive of any kind of *pure* expression that his interpretation didn't protect. When liberal critics brought up the issue of symbolic speech and demonstrations, my father was always quick to point out that the only cases where he denied First Amendment protection were those where an element of force was involved.

"What about picketing?" a law professor once asked Daddy. "Who can say that is ever anything more than pure expression?"

"I can," Hugo answered. "Let's take an extreme example. Did you ever see a fella on a labor picket line carrying a sign on a two by four with air holes cut in the sign? Well, I have. Is that speech? Or what about peacefully picketing someone's home? That isn't speech or press. That's like one of these nut telephone callers who keep calling you back time after time. There's nothing in the First Amendment says that one fella has the right to cram his opinions down another fella's throat. So far as I'm concerned, everything I've excluded from the definition has clearly involved to me something more than speech, press or peaceable assembly."

The press certainly had no reason to expect him to be their champion, considering the treatment he received at their hands during his lifetime. At one time or another, the press pictured him as a man who caused the deaths of Army Air Force pilots by exposing so much corruption in air mail subsidy contracts that the government was forced to take away air mail service from private airlines and turn it over to inexperienced Army pilots; as a brutal man who, by ruthlessly exposing corruption in public utility holding companies, caused holding company executives to commit suicide; as a man low enough to steam open the cook's mail to catch a lawyer-lobbyist; as a white racist; as a man too incompetent and too inexperienced to serve on the Supreme Court of the United States; as a Communist sympathizer; as a black nationalist; and, finally, as an old fogey reactionary. None of this ever embittered him. If anything, his confidence that the First Amendment protections were *the* key protections for our democratic republic became strengthened by these experiences.

This does not mean, however, that he approved of the concentration of power that has developed in the media. Breaking up and dispersing that power more equably would present a number of problems, he realized, since people would immediately cry censorship. But he insisted that the First Amendment had nothing to do with the problem of concentration of power; and that you had to be careful that economic power is the *real* reason for moving against these media empires, rather than some opinion they have just expressed. Admittedly, even when Daddy stated flatly "no law" meant no law, the problems concerning the First Amendment remained complex indeed.

Besides the First Amendment, Daddy's other main concern on the Court was certiorari. Whenever I think of Daddy inside the Supreme Court building, I can see him hurrying down the marble hall with his beat-up felt hat slapped down on his head, whistling "All Policemen Have Big Feet," and carrying his battered briefcase stuffed almost to the point of bursting with certiorari petitions.

These certiorari petitions play a big role in the life of any Supreme Court Justice. If four Justices vote to hear a case on the basis of these petitions, it is placed on the docket, fully briefed and then argued orally. When Daddy first came on the Court, the vote on these certiorari petitions was secret. He and Justice Douglas, however, forced the Court to publicize the vote on them.

My father recognized the process of selecting cases as the heart of a Justice's job, for he believed that whoever has the power to decide what cases will appear has the power of the Court and this was therefore not a function to be relegated to clerks or anybody else. Felix Frankfurter and other Justices had complained about the workload this entailed, but Daddy insisted that an experienced judge should be able to weed out the frivolous cases with five minutes' skimming of the briefs and a law clerk's notes. And after all, he told me, it was Bill Douglas and he who always voted to grant the most petitions, thereby creating more work for themselves and the other Justices. Yet they never felt there was a problem of overwork.

Daddy used to keep up with his certiorari by reading them whenever he had a spare moment—at his desk, in the bathroom, on the tennis court, in the car or in bed when he had insomnia. Through his own personal review, he kept up with the doings of the courts of appeal and the district courts, and with the actions of certain judges who were regularly overturning jury verdicts, rendering judgments without trial, mistreating lawyers, tricking people into pleas of guilty, or imposing their own views of right and wrong on the community. "They got awesome power, Son. If we don't watch them, nobody will. The Congress watches us, but they can't watch them. Some of them puff up like kings, and we're the only thing standing between them and their victims."

Daddy always regarded the Court as an untouchable institution, and he aimed to keep it that way and make it more so if he could. He felt it was extremely important that the people have full confidence in the integrity of at least one branch of the government, and he believed that the Court deserved this confidence because it has been relatively free of corruption. For example, he pointed out that even though advance knowledge of a decision could make someone a millionaire if he played the stock market right, no judge, clerk, printer or messenger, so far as he knew, had ever used this information to his own advantage. Since it was paramount that the action of each Justice should be above suspicion, Daddy always asked me to warn him about any case I could benefit from directly or indirectly. Although Charles Evans Hughes had sat when his son argued, even with this precedent and the knowledge that he would probably rule fairly, Daddy was aware that it was important to avoid any situation that could give rise to suspicion about his impartiality.

Hugo never tolerated any attempt to approach him other than by official Court filings or oral argument in the Court. Once a lawyer friend of mine brought a client for whom he had filed a petition for certiorari to 619 South Lee Street. Daddy would not let him in and after that he never even acknowledged that the lawyer existed. Another time a man, who theretofore had enjoyed a particularly close relationship with my father, approached him and another Justice. The other Justice was for this lawyer's client, Hugo against. After this meeting, Hugo and the other Justice agreed that Hugo would stay on the case, and the other Justice would get out; as a result this swung the vote against the lawyer's client. The offender learned that it does not pay to try to influence the Supreme Court by improper means, and, of course, Daddy would have absolutely nothing to do with him afterwards.

Daddy's concern that the Court also be free from any suspicion of Presidential influence lost him one beloved friend on the Court and brought down on his head the only accusation of misconduct ever made against him. When he was first appointed to the Court, my father tried by one means or another to advise the President on important matters. But he soon reached the conclusion that the job of Supreme Court Justice was inconsistent with the job of Presidential adviser. The founders intended the two departments to be separate, he realized, and advising the President just didn't square with that principle. Of course, he never stopped thinking that the executive branch would fare much better if its officers listened to him, but he did stop advising. As a result he looked askance at any Supreme Court Justice serving as an executive or Presidential officer on leave of absence from the Court, and he made no secret of his disapproval. No matter who the appointee, he complained openly and vigorously.

When President Roosevelt appointed Owen J. Roberts to chair the Pearl Harbor Commission, Daddy disapproved and made his position known to all the brethren on the Court, including Justice Roberts. Daddy had always been very close to Justice Roberts personally, even though their views did not very often coincide. They had a good time together, and their sense of humor blended. But when Roberts returned, he treated Hugo in a very distant manner. It hurt Daddy, for he truly loved and respected Owen Roberts. Try as he would, Daddy could never reestablish his pre-Pearl Harbor Commission relationship with Justice Roberts.

When President Truman chose Justice Robert Jackson to be the chief prosecutor at the Nuremberg trials, Daddy also made his opposition known. Hugo felt that Jackson would make an excellent chief prosecutor, but he felt strongly that Jackson had no business taking a leave of absence from his job on the Supreme Court to undertake an executive function. It not only subverted the separation of powers, but it also crippled the ability of the Court to function at full capacity.

No doubt this open hostility to Jackson's service at Nuremberg was part of the reason for the attack Jackson unleashed at Daddy from Germany, but to Daddy the bolt came out of a clear blue sky. Jackson accused Daddy of wrongdoing for sitting on a case which had been argued by General H. Lee Randolph, Daddy's former law partner. Daddy dismissed the accusation as silly because he and the General had parted company long ago over the General's proclivity for gambling. In addition, Daddy suspected that the General had aided and abetted Daddy's enemies in publishing the Ku Klux Klan material. If anything other than neutral, Daddy's inclinations would have been to rule against the General.

Because the accusations were absurd, Daddy kept his ears open and found out what had been the real cause of Justice Jackson's attack. Chief Justice Harlan Fiske Stone had died shortly before the incident, leaving the job of Chief Justice open. Apparently, as an inducement to get Jackson to go to Nuremberg, the President had promised him this position; and even without this promise, he appeared to be the logical choice. But then, Fred Vinson got the job, and Jackson blamed Daddy.

It seemed that somebody had represented to Justice Jackson that Daddy had told President Truman he would resign if Jackson was named Chief Justice. It was a plain lie. Daddy had said no such thing. We never knew who had been responsible for the misinformation that was passed to Justice Jackson. It was reported that Justice Frankfurter had told Jackson that it was Hugo who had made this threat.

At that time, however, Daddy and I were working very hard on improving our tennis game and Daddy had no time for plotting and scheming. He was much more interested in developing more top spin on his forehand.

"Whatever it is, Son, I don't want to make any more of it, it will pass. It is silly, silly stuff. This Court doesn't need any public rows among its judges." He refused to comment to the papers, despite a veritable siege of the house by reporters. "Tell 'em I said, 'No comment,' Son," and that is what I did.

When Justice Jackson returned from Germany, Daddy treated him as if nothing had ever happened. In later years, they appeared to have become much closer than they had ever been before. Just a couple of days before Justice Jackson died, he visited Daddy in his office, and these two old trial lawyers had a lively time trying to top each other's courtroom stories.

With all the hell Daddy would raise about a Justice placing himself in a compromising position in regard to a President, I always marveled at his calm acceptance of what Congress did to the Supreme Court to coerce the Justices into ruling more in accord with the precepts of a conservative legislative branch. Shortly after the Court handed down the decision ordering the end of segregation in the schools *(Brown v. Board of Education)* in 1954, the salaries of the Justices began to lag behind those of other branches of the government. When I remarked, "That's a dirty trick," Daddy replied, "Son, that's the separation of powers. That's people, that's the system, that's politics. We rule contrary to their notions, they tinker with our salaries."

When Daddy died, his widow's pension was only $5,-000 in contrast to $12,500 for the widow of a brand-new United States district judge. One congressman told me, "We don't intend to let some young girl hit the jackpot by marrying Justice Douglas." If Daddy had been alive, I know he would have laughed and told me, "It's not the young girls, Son. It's Bill's views—and not just his. Let's not kid ourselves. It's mine too."

A Most
Difficult Task

❧

A couple of years after Mama died, Daddy contracted shingles, a disease of the skin affecting the nerves and marked by blisters. It proved to be a great trial for him, for it seemed as if nobody could be more sensitive to pain than he was. Shingles on a man nearly seventy years of age is like putting him on a torture rack—with Daddy, it was worse. It started on his hips and moved down his legs to his feet, causing him months of almost unbearable pain. He could not sleep, his face was always tense, his teeth clenched together, and much of the time he hissed and moaned. Unfortunately, he could not tolerate the pain-killing drugs prescribed for him; they literally made him sick to his stomach or tore up his nervous system. So I made him try liquor. Bourbon, scotch, rum—nothing worked until he tested gin. His pain was so intense and gruesome that sometimes he would down a whole quart of gin, which relieved his pain and at the same time left him completely sober and eager to discuss a pending case with me. Much to his credit, when the shingles left he had no more interest in gin. He returned to his fear and hatred of liquor, so that only at his most restless moments did he indulge in a couple of ounces of bourbon before dinner.

Physical malfunction was Daddy's nemesis. He believed he could control everything else, whether he actually could or not, but he felt too much was out of his own hands when it came to being sick, and this terrified him. A common cold knocked him for a loop, even when he was a young, healthy man. He would go to bed and either sleep or just stare vacantly about. It was almost as if he felt each cold was the end—that his last illness had come.

But as big a baby as he was about a cold, he had real fortitude about more serious problems. From the time he was fifty years old, X-rays of his back showed serious arthritic deformation. He never complained, even though you could see him wincing with back pain after two or three hours of tennis. Sometimes he would play tennis with both knees swollen with fluid. On these occasions, he would excuse himself, walk into the bathroom and stick a needle in his knees to drain off the fluid.

Although Daddy really had fine health most of the time, he was constantly plagued by little nitty things such as his prostate, which was operated on when he was in his early sixties. In the family, we joked about it because of the story Daddy always used to tell: "You should never buy a cheap bicycle. That's what ruined my prostate. When I was a boy I scrimped and saved and got up ten dollars to send off for this bicycle. When it came, the seat was too high for me. But I rode it anyhow. It rubbed me so that it injured my prostate. Man, how I scrimped and saved for that bicycle. And now look what it got me."

Another minor affliction that he periodically suffered

from was fever blisters cropping up around his mouth. Nothing would cure them except some awful white ointment. His vanity was such that he did not want to be outside the house with that stuff on, so he would stay home and work until the blisters went away.

One day I was surprised to learn that until recently Daddy hadn't been aware how much hair he had lost. "I always had the image of a heavy head of hair back around my crown," he told me. "Then I saw a picture of the back of my head at the wedding of Justice Roberts' daughter. That saucer around my crown almost made me cry."

Going bald, minor illnesses, these things concerned him not so much because his vanity was offended, but—I believe—because they were signs of losing control, something that he always feared. Right after he recovered from his terrible bout with shingles, which might have brought these fears to a head, he called me into his study.

"Son, the years are flying by, they go so fast."

"That's true, Daddy."

"Aah, you don't know yet. You just don't know."

"What's on your mind?" I said.

"I'm worried, Son. I have such an important job. I'm worried about getting old."

"Ah, Daddy," I fired back. "If anything, you're better able to handle your job than you have ever been."

"I know that, but I'm worried about the future. Holmes, Brandeis, Cardozo—they all sat too long. I think nature will tell me when I ought to get off, but I'm not so sure. Those fellas were pretty good men in their day themselves. Nature didn't tell *them* when to get off."

"Well, nature will tell you, Daddy."

"I can't be sure, Son. I want you to watch me—you've

got to watch my mind, my energy, my eyes, my ears, my judgment."

"What are you talking about?"

"Just what I said, Son. Old judges go to sleep on the bench, old men speak too long, old men drive cars when they shouldn't. I want you to promise to deal with me on these things."

"Daddy," I said, "you won't listen to me. You're being too hard on me charging me with that."

He paused a moment, then said, "Son, I've tried to keep you from being a hero worshipper, and I think I have— with one exception."

"I know—that's you."

"Right. So whatever you say about me, I know you think it's right, because if there's anything wrong between us it's because you think too much of me."

"What if you jump on me?"

"I probably will, but I'm charging you with this task. If I don't agree, and I'm eighty, that's your problem. You've got to stop me from doing what I ought not to do, if it ever comes to that."

I wish I had recorded this conversation and the many similar ones we had later, because I had a tough time carrying out this new responsibility. The first time I saw him in danger of giving a too lengthy speech, I held up my watch after twenty minutes, the time limit he had given me for lunch and dinner speeches. He paid not a jot of attention to me. Five minutes later I held it up again, and still he did not respond. Two minutes later I held it up yet again, and he kept right on talking. To make a long story short, he defied me completely. He won this round, since even his enemies praised the speech and jumped all over me for trying to stop him.

But then reports began coming back to me about speeches that lasted as long as two hours. I reminded Daddy once again, but as far as I could see he did not do anything about it. Before his last speech in San Antonio, Texas, to the Fifth Circuit Judicial Conference, I once again performed my duty before he mounted the rostrum.

"Daddy, my speaking teacher told me twenty minutes."

His temper flared: "Son, I'm sick of this. You don't know what it's like to be old."

I went over and stroked him on the head and said, "Maybe I'd have had an independent view if my teacher hadn't brainwashed me." Although the speech seemed too long, I am sure it was a whole lot shorter than it would have been without the confrontation.

His charge to watch his driving proved to be an even more difficult responsibility. Because he had insisted on driving down to Florida one Christmas vacation when I wasn't sure he could really drive anymore, I decided to come up to Washington and help him drive down. We started out with me at the wheel, but every time we stopped he would insist on driving, even though his eyesight had deteriorated quite badly that winter. I kept stalling him until finally, knowing the risk to our lives, I decided it might do him a lot of good and let him take over. He whipped his big Buick around dangerously on and off the shoulder of the road and once we almost wound up in a corn field. When I could stand it no longer and asked him to let me take over again, he was infuriated. "Son, I will never drive again with you in the car. You are wrong, very wrong. I *can* drive all right. You don't take into account a lot of factors—"

"Sir," I said, "I am only doing what you told me to do many years ago—"

But he still would not believe me. He acted as if he thought I was trying to deny his manhood, and he never again asked to drive when I was in the car, although he was still able to intimidate others.

One night after the Florida trip, he bulldozed Spencer into allowing him to take the wheel on the way home from work. Two and a half blocks down the road from the Supreme Court building, he got to a very narrow street, where he banged into a parked car. That was the end; he never drove again or asked to drive again. But that didn't prevent him from becoming a militant back-seat driver. According to him, nobody at the wheel did anything right, and nobody knew the way to any place. All of us had a bad time, but Spencer had the worst. At a stoplight he would say, "O.K., Spencer, you got it. Cut out." On the freeway: "Spencer, these days they never stop. The cars keep coming, you've got to force in, don't be so bashful. Now gun into that hole."

No matter what lane Spencer drove in, Daddy always complained that it was the wrong one. At the Fourteenth Street Bridge, as you come from Alexandria into Washington, you are supposed to be in the right lanes to go into town. One morning, when I was riding with Daddy and Spencer, Daddy felt he was running very late and literally forced Spencer to stay in the extreme left lane, where he could go faster. "Judge," Spencer said, "I can't turn into town on the Fourteenth Street Bridge if I do."

"Sure you can, they'll let us in up there. There are always some nice people in a line of traffic."

"Not to somebody that's scooting ahead on the outside lane, Judge."

"Do it, Spencer."

Spencer did, but there were no nice people.

"Force your way in—" Instead, Spencer gunned the car forward. "Spencer, you're passing the Fourteenth Street Bridge! Spencer, you're heading for Memorial Bridge!" Daddy yelled.

"Judge," said Spencer, "I had to do it, that man behind just kept plowing straight ahead into us—"

Daddy looked at me and said, "Son, Spencer just can't drive. He's too cautious. Now I'm going to be late."

Bad as he was about speeches and driving, he never failed on important matters. Although he never fell asleep on the bench, the fear that he might probably contributed to a change of policy regarding the questioning of lawyers during their argument. For most of his career, he would usually limit himself to one or two questions that went straight to the heart of the issue. But in his last years he asked more questions and he asked them with more vigor, so much so that one day I commented, "Are you sure you're not doing some of that questioning just to provoke the feeling, 'Man, that old man is sure alert'?"

He dismissed this with "I'm not asking any more questions than I always have." But he was.

With my father's knowledge and consent, I observed his work meticulously during these years, checking with his clerks and other Justices, as well as talking with lawyers who argued before the Supreme Court, law school professors, doctors and his secretary. There was never any doubt about his ability to carry out his job until 1970. The first sign of failing health appeared one day when he was on the tennis court, right after the summer adjournment of the Court; he became dizzy and blacked out. After he had been taken into the house and revived, he was driven to the hospital. The doctors reported that he had had a slight stroke, but they sent him right back home, saying that although he was a little confused now, he would be able to make a good recovery.

I was in Miami when all this happened, but after receiving a phone call from 619 South Lee Street, I told Daddy that by "chance" I had to be in Washington on business the next day. When I arrived I saw that he was very concerned.

"Shut the door, Son," he said. "Something bad happened to me out there on the tennis court. My mind is sluggish—the connections don't come in a flash and I don't have the confidence in my memory. Do you think I ought to get off the Court?"

"It's too early to tell, Daddy."

After a few days of watching over him closely, I went back South, but found reasons to call him three or four times a week. As time went by, his voice began to sound young again, he became more positive in his outlook, and when I prodded him, he came right back with a strong reply. Finally, on one call he said, "Son, I got to make up my mind about retirement."

"I know, Daddy. I've got to be up in Washington soon. I thought I'd bring the family."

"Good," he said.

When we arrived, I contacted his doctors and they told me, "He has come back. There is a little impairment. But it would almost be treason to let him retire. He still has the ability to function well, to an extraordinary degree."

Again, Daddy and I had another private session in his study. "What do you think? Has this thing affected me so I'm not the same?"

I answered him frankly, "Yes, it has, Daddy."

"Well, I guess I ought to get off the Court then—"

"I didn't say that."

"Yes, you did," he said peevishly.

"You misunderstood, Daddy. I said you were not the old Hugo Black anymore. I didn't say you weren't still a Supreme Court superstar when it comes to ability to judge soundly and push out quality and quantity production. It just may not come as easy as it did before."

"You sure that isn't sentiment, son?"

"There's no room for that in what we're discussing. The country is involved. How many times have you told me you aren't going to leave me any material things—just the legacy of what you've done and your views. I wouldn't think of giving up a legacy like that."

Tears welled up in his eyes. "I believe you wouldn't, Son, much as you'd hate to hurt me. But I'm not sure you're right."

"You asked for my opinion, Daddy, you got it. I know you're the one who has to decide. You can't delegate that responsibility."

After giving the matter a good deal of thought, Daddy finally decided to stay on the Court. I do not think he ever regretted this decision because great opinions followed, as well as great speeches—even if they were a little too long.

Hugo Marries
Again

One day in 1956 Daddy phoned me and said that his secretary, Gladys Coates, was retiring. He asked me to look around in Alabama for someone to replace her—a Southern woman had extra grace and charm, he said. He wanted someone who could not only type and take shorthand, but also have an easy friendliness that would make people feel comfortable.

The first person I contacted was Mary Tortoricci, who was then the first assistant clerk in the federal court. Although she would have been fine for the job, she had a son in Birmingham and wanted to stay near him. Mary recommended Elizabeth DeMeritte, her favorite assistant, and after speaking highly of her abilities, she added, "Elizabeth has a son in Washington and she wants to leave her husband. She just stayed with her husband all these years to get their son raised."

"Well, Mary," I said, "Daddy is single. I don't want him involved in any divorce."

"She is going to do it anyhow," Mary said. "She's right for the job."

First thing I knew, Colonel Bob Bradford, one of my father's main supporters from north Alabama and an Assistant United States Attorney, called me recommending Elizabeth. Then Judge Seyborne Lynne in Birmingham got in touch with me and he, too, recommended Elizabeth in the highest terms; he assured me that there would be no problem because of her divorce—the differences she had with her husband were well known and nobody would blame Daddy for anything that happened. After receiving these assurances, I arranged for Elizabeth to have an interview with Daddy. From there on, she was on her own. She got the job, and she got her divorce shortly thereafter.

It was not long before I noticed that Daddy was beginning to behave somewhat peculiarly. At this time when he was single it was my habit to call him long distance three times a week, and he would always be waiting for these calls. After Elizabeth arrived, he would often not be there to answer the phone. When I would finally contact him and tell him we had missed talking to him, his explanation would sound mighty fishy. He even told me once he had been to a baseball game. There just was no way he was ever going to any baseball game!

When I had to go to Washington on business, I always went right to the house and stayed there. After Elizabeth became his secretary, he would come in at an hour that was very late for him—eleven-thirty or twelve. I would say, "Hi, Daddy, where've you been?"

He would say, "To a movie."

I knew that was not true, because he didn't like movies at all.

Once, he even said to me, "To a hockey game." Now, I knew that was a whopping lie.

So I nosed about to see what was going on, and it didn't take long to find out that he was going out with Elizabeth. It was all around town. Whenever I saw her, I knew she wanted to tell me something, but she looked scared. It was really stupid, his trying to deceive me. Nevertheless I pretended that I believed him, and he didn't have the sensitivity to know he was not fooling me. I wondered what in the world was making him sneaky with me when in the past he had always been forthright. Graham and I could come up with only one answer. It had to be Mama. He thought that I would resent his having anything to do with another woman because of my reverence for her. So I just waited.

The time came. He phoned me long distance one day, and he said in a most hostile, belligerent tone: "Son, I'm getting married to Elizabeth tomorrow. I thought you ought to know."

Silence.

"Well, Daddy," I said, "aren't you even going to ask me to be best man? After all, I found her for you."

Silence.

"Would you be, Son?"

"You bet. What time tomorrow?"

"Four in the afternoon."

"O.K., I'll be there in the morning."

The next day he and Elizabeth were married in the living room of the house at 619 South Lee Street by the Reverend A. Powell Davies, of the Unitarian Church, the same man who had delivered a beautiful eulogy at Mama's funeral.

I am sure the marriage added at least ten years to his life. With Elizabeth there as a combination secretary, nurse, companion and lover, I no longer had to call him three times a week. He confided proudly to me that with her he was almost as much a man as he had ever been. Elizabeth brought friends into the house by arranging parties, and although Daddy always complained about these social evenings, I am sure he really enjoyed them—coaxed along by Elizabeth he would have a grand time entertaining the guests by playing the piano and the harmonica and singing old songs. But more important, Elizabeth applauded his diligence and showed pride in his work. She really made those last years for him, and I am proud that I had something to do with bringing it about.

Leaving
Alabama

As much as my father wanted anything, he would have liked me to follow in his footsteps in politics. Although he always tried to convince me and himself that he let me make my own decisions, when it came to selecting a college, he worked on me to attend the University of Alabama. "Son," he said, "if you go to the University of Alabama, you will make a lot of friends all over the state. If you should decide to go into politics, they can really help you." I leaned toward an Ivy League school, but in the end I decided to go to the University of Alabama because I knew he wanted me to.

When I graduated from law school at Yale and returned to Alabama to practice law, I definitely had politics in mind. Daddy and I had a plan. I would await an opportunity to run for the congressional seat from Birmingham, capture that, then wait for Lister Hill or John Sparkman to retire or die and go for a seat in the United States Senate. From there, who knows? My political base would be Daddy's old friends and their children, my friends at the university and the members of several labor unions whom Buddy and I represented.

At first, it appeared that our plan would go well. Organizations of all types invited me to speak and the speeches went well. Daddy's old friends advised and guided me along, while his enemies regarded me as public enemy number one. There was one drawback, though: only whites had the vote at that time, thanks to, among others, my grandfather, Dr. Sterling J. Foster, who had served as a registrar of voters and sanctimoniously administered literacy tests of sufficient difficulty to disqualify every black man. Both Buddy and I would speak cordially to the black lawyers in Birmingham and even shake hands with them. We would not necessarily believe a white man over a black man, and we would become enraged when some white bully tried to lord it over a black man. But in our relations with black people we were discreet enough so that our non-racist attitude could not hurt too much if one of us "offered for office"—Buddy was actually less discreet and more courageous than I.

A chance to capture the congressional seat came when the incumbent decided to run for the United States Senate. I did not have to be aggressive to offer for the now vacant seat in the House. Luther Patrick, who had once held the seat, came to me and said I should run. Senator Hill also inquired about my interest, as well as many friends of mine. Before I made any decision, I called Daddy to get his advice. I was surprised and a little alarmed by his answer. He told me he had something very important to talk to me about, and asked me to fly up to Washington. I agreed and decided to go that same day. When I got to the house, Daddy took me into his study and said, "This is your chance, Son. But I've got to tell you something in the strictest of confidence that has a lot to do with your decision."

"What's that, Daddy?"

"We've got some cases up before us where they are challenging segregation of the races. I agree with old Justice Harlan's dissent in *Plessy v. Ferguson.* I don't believe segregation is constitutional."

"I think you are right, Daddy."

"But don't you see what that will do to you? Maybe you can make it this time, but they will get you next time, unless, of course, you are willing to abuse the Supreme Court."

"For what, Daddy? I agree and besides, even if I didn't, I wouldn't jump on you."

"I know that, Son, but you wouldn't have to get after me—just the Court."

"I couldn't."

"You understand, Son. I've got to do it even though it's going to mess up your plans."

"You've got to, Daddy. I wouldn't have any respect for you if you didn't. What should I tell Luther and the others?"

"I don't know," Daddy said.

But by the time I got back to Alabama, I had made up my mind. I told them I was not ready. Being politicians, they were puzzled, and suspected rightly that I knew something they did not.

Daddy knew what he was talking about. In *Brown v. Board of Education,* the Court did unanimously hold that segregation of the races in public schools was unconstitutional, and they stated that public schools must be desegregated "with all deliberate speed." I knew that the term "all deliberate speed" disturbed Daddy. "It tells the enemies of the decision that for the present the status quo will do and gives them time to contrive devices to stall off segregation." But he could not bring the Court to abandon unanimously the critical phrase. And Daddy was not about to do anything to fragment the Court in that landmark opinion. He felt that the decision represented revolution in the South and that everything would be accomplished with less resistance if the Court unanimously agreed that the opinion represented the law.

His fears about the reaction proved to be well founded. All hell broke loose in the Birmingham community. Politicians who had given me wholehearted support before were now very cool. Indeed, the situation was such that if a candidate had an opponent who merely maintained silence about the Supreme Court, he had a sure road to victory by claiming that by his silence his opponent was condoning the Court's action. Most of the newspapers, politicians and citizens of Hugo's homestate looked on Daddy as "a traitor to the South," and a candidate for governor opined one day that "Justice Black is not fit to try a chicken thief."

Truth to tell, I ran into few people who treated my family discourteously. In my professional life, however, I did encounter some problems. When one lawyer tried to use Daddy to prejudice the jury against my client, I told the jury:

"Gentlemen, the defendant's lawyer is a desperate man. He can't find any decent arguments against our case. He can't find a reason to knock my client or even me. So he has chosen to defend this case by not-so-subtle references to my daddy, who used to be your United States senator and is now on the Supreme Court of the United States. The defendant's lawyer indicates you ought to bring in a verdict for his client because my daddy is too much for colored people. Well, gentlemen, let's talk about my daddy. I know one thing about him. As far as I'm concerned he is the greatest daddy in the world. He has been in politics forty years. How many of you have ever heard whispers that he made money at the public's expense or disgraced you by public misconduct or ruled on a case on the basis of anything but his conscience? Is there a one of you who could ask for anything more than to have him sit on your case if you were weak or helpless or had the whole world against you? Oh, true, yesterday, the colored people said he was too much for white people. Now the white people say he is too much for colored people. Who knows, maybe tomorrow the colored people will be saying he is too much for white people. But gentlemen, can you imagine how proud I am of my daddy when after forty years of politics, the most anybody can scrape up in the way of bad things against him is that Hugo Black is too much for this or that? Now, please, go out there and show these fellows that you resent somebody trying to win a case against a man on the basis that the lawyer he selected has Judge Hugo Black for a daddy." And the jury did just that. Until the day I left Alabama, nobody ever brought up anything else like that before a jury in any of my cases.

Occasionally, of course, some nitwit would come up to me on the street and say, "How many niggers did you eat with last night?" I would laugh and say something like "Last night was slow—just seven."

Whenever Daddy came into town, there were problems. Invariably someone would insult him on the street by saying, "You are a traitor to the South," or some such nonsense. He would just smile, grab the offender by the hand and say, "Glad to have your views." Then several times during the day and night we would get anonymous phone calls from people who blurted out brilliant things like "Hugo Black is a nigger lover."

Once in the midst of all this unpleasantness, Daddy kidded me by saying, "The roughnecks who do that need you and Buddy to defend them when they use violence to win a strike." But to some extent, his kidding had some truth in it. I remember when some drunken, hot-headed white fools attacked Nat King Cole in the Birmingham Auditorium right in the middle of a song. I was called and asked to represent them by the ex-president of a local union of the United Steelworkers. When Daddy heard of this, he said jokingly, "That's because they know you are the greatest mob lawyer in America."

Although my family was blackballed from many country clubs and other organizations, I do not believe that Daddy's position on race had as much to do with it as the fact that I supported labor unions. In this role, Buddy and I constantly encountered the city's establishment in an area most sensitive to them, and invariably they felt that we had betrayed our class and all law-abiding people. But this same alliance helped me out in the courtroom, since the juries were usually made up of people in unions we represented. And, no doubt, it protected my family from violence. Once, I received an anonymous call saying that a cross would be burned in my yard that night, but nothing happened. The next day I learned that a friend of mine, whom we had successfully defended against a charge of violence while he was on strike, had let it be known that if a cross burned in my yard the perpetrators would not live until morning.

Even at this time when Daddy appeared to be a hateful renegade, he still knew exactly what would appeal to a Jefferson County jury. Buddy and I had a case for a black man who had gone North to Detroit to live, and on a visit to his family in Alabama he had been injured. The insurance company would pay nothing because they were sure the all-white jury's feelings would run high against the plaintiff. When I asked Daddy for advice he told me: "Just tell your man to act like Southern white people expect him to act and when they start the race stuff, you tell the jury you would rather have a case like this here in Birmingham than anywhere else in America. Tell them to send the message back to *Dee*-troit and Chicago and New York that we take better care of this kind of a plaintiff than anybody else in America." My client reluctantly accepted my suggestion that he act as Jefferson County white people would expect a "good nigger" to act, and then I used Daddy's argument. The jury returned a verdict much higher, I am sure, than a jury would have in Detroit.

As time went on, the pressure didn't let up on me and my family. Whenever I could make light of the problems we faced, I did, just to ease the burden. Once a bigoted politician whom I nevertheless liked immensely called and said, "Hugo, would you be offended if I took a crack at your daddy?" I laughed and replied, "I'd do anything for you, even come out against you if it would help."

But things were getting bad. A black lawyer friend said to me one day, "Hugo, you should stop shaking my hand when you see me. It just hurts you and we don't want you hurt." When it came time for jury selection, the bailiff would say, "We got four up there in this group. Shall I just leave them?" And I would nod yes.

Incidents of violence and oppression were occurring quite frequently—events that turned my stomach. Once, I would have been eager to help the victims, but now I found myself refusing. When Fred Shuttlesworth, who was black, tried to ride in the front of a bus, a certain judge heard the case against Fred on a Thursday night. Never sober after twelve noon, this man prided himself on his knowledge of "niggers" and, as a lawyer, represented only black people. He always wore spats over his shoes because, in his words, "Nothin' impresses a nigger like spats." In order to frustrate Fred's appeal and stay during appeal, he said after hearing the evidence, "I can't make up my mind. Take the nigger to jail until I come back Tuesday night." After Fred's black lawyers failed to get bail or habeas corpus, they asked prominent white lawyers for help, all of whom refused. Then the lawyers came to me, and after considering it I refused on the ground that my representation "would hurt more than it would help." But in my heart I felt I was copping out. Around that same time a black lawyer friend asked me to sponsor him for the American and Birmingham bar associations, and I had to refuse on the same grounds that my support would only hurt him.

When *The New York Times* asked me to defend them against the ridiculous "libel" suit filed by Bull Connor and others, I at first tentatively agreed. But when neighbors heard of this they said, "Hugo, you aren't going to represent *The New York Times* against us, are you? You're not gonna turn against us like your daddy?" After a conference with my partners, I requested the *Times* to pay my fee in advance, knowing full well that they would not agree to this. When they did refuse payment in advance, I felt ashamed of myself, but relieved. By this time, Daddy would not come down to Alabama to visit us because he knew it would only cause trouble.

Events like these began making me feel more and more unhappy. Finally, a little incident occurred that was, for me, the last straw. Returning one day from Tuscaloosa, where I had just won a big victory, I went to tell my partners, Buddy and Bill, the good news. When my secretary told me they were out trying a jury case for a black man, I drove down to the courthouse, and then peered through the glass panes of the doors to the courtroom to see if I could get their attention. Buddy saw me and immediately stood up and asked for a recess. Bill and he then came out, and Bill said to me, "Go back to the office. They are trying to make you an issue. Don't let them see you."

I knew then that I had to get out. We were being so intimidated by the feeling against Daddy that I knew my partners would be better off without me and I would be more effective somewhere else. I realized I could not keep my self-respect if I kept running from the just side of fights. And I felt that I did not want to live any place where my daddy, who should have been respected beyond all other Alabama public figures, living or dead, could not come without being treated like a leper.

Although our law firm was reportedly one of the top earners among Birmingham attorneys, I felt that my financial future was limited in Birmingham in comparison with what it could become in a more dynamic area. Then, too, I was just plain embarrassed for a lot of people I loved. On television one night I watched a friend of mine who had supported Daddy in the Klu Klux Klan crisis defend segregation to a nationwide audience with this "biological fact": "Why, did you ever watch chickens in the barnyard? The black chickens cluster together. They don't want to be around the white chickens. That's just nature." On another national television program, another friend, at the urging of a national commentator, read different parts of the Bible to show why we had to keep our whites separated from the blacks. It was just too much.

After considering the pros and cons of various cities, I decided to move to Miami, a place Daddy loved to visit. Although it meant starting over again, the economic opportunity was there, because, much as California had prospered in previous years, Miami's population and economy were growing at a tremendous rate. Most of all, it was populated by people from all over the country, but, unlike California, was full of Southerners or "crackers," as they are called in Florida. And despite everything, I wanted "crackers" around me. When I told Daddy I was afraid because there were thousands of lawyers in Dade County, he tried to reassure me by saying, "Son, there is always room at the top."

When the news got out that I was leaving Alabama, the reaction was mixed. The Alabama *Journal* carried this editorial, full of misinformation but still encasing a kernel of truth:

HUGO BLACK, JR., son of the notorious justice of the U.S. Supreme Court, studied law at the University of Alabama and went to his home city and opened offices to practice his profession. It didn't work out. The name he bore was anathema in Birmingham.

He had to suffer for the sins of his father. He had to be a pariah in the city where his father had practiced law for enough years to be making $50,000 a year before mounting a flivver and covering the state in a campaign for U.S. Senator. The father was elected by the Ku Klux Klan, and his reputation as a senator or at least his regularity in following the FDR line won an appointment to the Supreme Court by the New Deal bull of the woods. The father's record on the court has been so obnoxious that it is disastrous to the son.

Hugo Junior has picked up and left town. The word is that he has taken his family to California and will try out there to see if a man bearing the name Hugo Black can live in peace and comfort and make a living in the practice of law.

Although I am sure many people thought Good riddance, there were also the Dixiecrats who came to me with tears in their eyes offering me their help. There were those who said, "Hugo, don't go. Hugo Black is our treasure. You're all that we have left of him. Reconsider." Or, "Don't go, Hugo. You're the only one who can make fun out of this goddamned ugly conflict." And some other dear friend said, "Hugo, we have to lie low now. But the day will come. Stay. He's our finest, don't take what's left of him away."

When our friends finally accepted the fact that we were leaving, they called their friends in Miami and recommended us to them in the most flattering terms. If it had not been for those Alabamians who believed in Daddy and me when I left, I would be just another middle-aged rebel who jumped from a place where the grass was plenty green to a place where the grass looked greener from afar, but when you got to it, turned out to be dust.

Starting Over
in Florida

Anyone who intends to practice law in Florida must pass the Florida bar exam, no matter how many other states have licensed him. With my very busy practice in Birmingham, there seemed to me no way I could study for that bar exam and still do my share of work in our law firm. My situation on December 31, 1961, was not exactly enviable. I found myself without a job in Alabama, with no license to practice law in Florida nor any hope of obtaining one until October of 1962, and having only the most sparse connections, political or otherwise, with the exception of the names of Miami people who were friends of friends of mine.

But I did have a plan. By inquiring around I soon discovered that I could practice in Miami without being a member of the Florida bar if I represented the United States government. I knew I had the qualifications. There were two ways I could go about securing this employment: either I could be hired locally by the United States Attorney, or the Department of Justice could hire me as a special assistant to the Attorney General and send me in from Washington to supplement the staff of the Attorney. After failing to get employment on the local level, I went to work for the Department of Justice in the Tort Claims Division in Washington, D.C., with the understanding that I would be dispatched to Florida to help clear up a heavy trial backlog there.

On January 5, 1962, I left my family in Birmingham and moved in with Daddy and Elizabeth at 619 South Lee Street. For three months I worked hard at the Department of Justice while studying for the Florida bar at night. By March, however, it became evident that the master plan had run into difficulty. When I inquired, I learned that the conservative federal politicians in Florida—who, in the final analysis, control the office of the United States Attorney—simply did not want me down there. They did not like my history of labor union representation, nor did they like the stories that I had left Alabama because of my tendencies toward economic and racial radicalism.

Seeing that this plan would never work out no matter how long I spent on it, I made arrangements to go to Florida and work in the office of one of Daddy's former clerks, Sam Daniels. Sam had recently separated from his wife, so he and I shared an inexpensive apartment while my family remained in Birmingham for the time being. The single living was cheap; often Sam and I each spent less than a dollar a day on food.

As soon as I got settled I began calling on all the people whose names my friends had given me. These new acquaintances were all extremely kind and generous, furnishing me with a great deal of material and spiritual support. My greatest stroke of luck came, however, when

I visited Wilbur MacDuff, the cousin of my milkman in Birmingham. Wilbur's father had been sheriff of Jefferson County, Alabama, and a strong supporter of Daddy in both his races for the Senate. I found out that Wilbur ran the Dade County Law Library and headed a corps of legal researchers for the local circuit court judges. When I informed him of my present circumstances, he immediately offered me the best paying position he had, and I accepted. The salary came to less than a quarter of what I had grown accustomed to, but with stringent economy, it would be enough to support myself and my family in Birmingham.

Wilbur has one of those remarkable memories that can recall the name of a legal case, the book and page number where it is located, and the substance of what it is about. Our minds functioned well together. Whatever proposition I needed, he had a citation for me. That is the way we worked. I supplied the pen; he supplied the legal authority. In my job I came to know and work with all the circuit judges and met many Dade County lawyers. Wilbur and I performed every service from finding cases in point, sitting in on trials as advisers, analyzing and synthesizing conferences with judges, furnishing suggested rulings on motions, to taking entire records and coming up with suggested opinions (what Wilbur and I called "lock and key" jobs). It was a fine interlude—indeed something of a luxury for an advocate; all we had to do was locate the right course of action and follow it. Although I did a full day's work, I continued to prepare for the bar exam, getting up at four A.M. and studying for three hours.

During this period some of the teaching that Daddy

had been giving me down through the years really took on meaning. Thanks to him, I had developed some self-discipline. When you are a legal research assistant, you do not swell up and try to act like something bigger, and I had learned that one might put his whole being into whatever he is doing, no matter what it is, and enjoy a sense of fulfillment. I had learned to live within my own means, which now was crucial if I were to succeed. And what he had taught me about staying in good physical condition helped me function efficiently, and in a good frame of mind.

As I drove myself through this difficult period, Daddy gave me more spiritual aid and comfort that any son could ever hope for. He also kept me from making a very big mistake. I had prepared a resumé to present to various law firms for possible employment. It was a good one, but when I showed it to Daddy, he looked at it for a moment and then tore it into a thousand pieces. "Son, I don't want you soliciting employment. You really should go out on your own, but if you don't want to do that, don't go into partnership on any basis other than equal or better for you."

I followed his advice. The lawyer whom I came to admire most was Leon D. Black, Jr., who practiced in a small firm called Kelly, Paige & Black. Leon has everything I wanted in a partner: ability and character, toughness, quickness, youth, ambition—he also shows the sweetest disposition toward those who are close to him of anyone this side of my late mother. We opened up shop on an equal basis just as soon as I received the news that I had passed the bar. I had decided not to take any cases within my specialty of labor law, since I wanted to break away from my Alabama label of "labor's boy." Yet I did not want to accept employment that would make me oppose my old friends in the unions. Fortunately, there appeared to be an area wide open for someone who could translate complicated matters into Hugo Black prose for a jury, and who was willing to spend some time researching the issues. The field of complicated litigation was just developing, a field that included the many faces of fraud, antitrust law, business law, will contests and the like. I moved right into this area of practice, while Leon began to concentrate on representing people whose property was being condemned by the state.

Since the day we opened shop, we have won many cases, made an excellent living, and kept ourselves in such a state of independence that we are free to resist any demands by a client if we feel he is wrong. It was a terribly difficult struggle, starting my career over in middle age with the responsibility of a family, and I'm not sure I could have made it if it hadn't been for the tough lessons Daddy had taught me when I was growing up.

FF

Daddy's views in relation to those of Justice Felix Frankfurter ("FF") will probably take up more space in the
history books than any other single aspect of Hugo's service on the Supreme Court. During their lifetimes, the
media frequently referred to Hugo as the intellectual
leader of the liberal wing of the Court ("Black's Army,"
according to one article) and to FF as that of the conservative wing of the Court ("Frankfurter's Army").

In the beginning, however, when FF came on the Court
in 1939, a couple of years after Daddy, he was anathema
to corporate board members. For many years, as a law
professor at Harvard, he had inspired some of the finest
young minds in America. FF knew intimately everyone in
the liberal intellectual establishment in America and England. Justice Oliver Wendell Holmes and Justice Louis
Brandeis, two of the renowned liberals in the history of
the Supreme Court, almost invariably accepted as their
clerks the graduates of Harvard Law School recommended by FF, and Franklin D. Roosevelt staffed many of

the key posts in his administration with graduates recommended by him. FF had also been a leader in trying to convince the world that Sacco and Vanzetti had been unjustly convicted and in rallying support for them.

The intellectual and political influence of FF was all the more remarkable because of his origin. He came to this country from Austria as a very young boy with very little knowledge of English; yet he became a master of the English language and spoke with not a trace of a foreign accent.

Although Jewish and small in stature, FF had the bearing of a Prussian general, always standing perfectly erect. He had a deeply cleft chin and wore a pince-nez. When he walked, he literally bounced; he moved in jerks, snapping his head about quickly, waving his hands and arms about with lightning speed, and darting forward in his chair to make a point. In a moderately high-pitched voice he would always speak with passion, firing words at his audience like bullets from a machine gun. As with Daddy, there was something about FF's manner that convinced you that he felt he had the answer, and this, in turn, acting on the universal craving for certainty, tended to make you feel that FF did indeed have the answer. And again, as with Daddy, there was something about FF's manner and speech that tended to make you believe that all your good, chivalric, higher aspirations required agreement with his beliefs.

When FF came on the Court, I believe that he expected to form an army which would include Daddy as a lieutenant. After all, FF could have thought, with some justification, This Black is a liberal and a Southerner from a common family with very little formal education who would be impressed by my associations; and this Black supported my appointment and has openly expressed admiration for me. So no sooner was FF appointed than he began to woo Daddy, as well as Mama and all of us kids.

And, of course, no sooner was FF appointed than Daddy decided to win him over to *his* own views. After all, Daddy probably reasoned, my views are right, and this fellow has exhibited extraordinarily good sense down through the years. The first wooing telephone calls probably crossed.

But this mutual enterprise was doomed to failure, for by nature neither Hugo nor FF had it in him to be a lieutenant. It was inevitable that each should eventually go his separate way, trying his best to proselytize every man who sat on the Court during the time they served together. And, of course, every time thereafter that the two agreed, each hoped that the other had finally become convinced of the error of his ways.

FF in the court of an absolute monarch would have quickly achieved the position of whatever the name for First Adviser happened to be, and he would have held on to it. He was singularly endowed with those talents that can capture one all-powerful man and hold him: he was ambitious; he was a bona fide member of the intellectual elite; he had a profound sense of history; he possessed a talent for flattery; and in general he was wise in those conspiratorial ways with which a man of supreme ability captures and holds a king. But some of these very same talents are self-defeating in a court where you yourself have direct power and must persuade at least four men with equal power to accomplish your will.

Nevertheless, no man ever tried harder to become First

Adviser to a multi-headed polity than did FF. He bounced up and down the marble halls of the Supreme Court seeking to enlist for his army each Justice, along with the Justices' wives, children, law clerks and even messengers. He sent his clerks as his disciples into the constitutional law chairs in universities all over the country. Assiduously cultivating scholars and commentators on the Supreme Court, he penned them flattering notes about their articles, promotions, weddings, or the births of babies; and he invited them to his office for a conversation when they appeared in the courtroom. A Justice who disagreed with FF might well expect an article critical of his position to appear in a law journal, and, strangely enough, the language might tend to resemble the very language FF had used in a private conference in which he had sought to bring the Justice around.

FF always felt strongly that the Supreme Court should limit its attention to important matters of state, and believed that the Court was accepting and reversing too many cases where a judge had taken away by post-trial order a jury verdict in favor of, say, an injured railroad worker under the Federal Employer's Liability Act (F.E.L.A.). Hugo was the moving force behind this practice. When FF could not bring about its end, he cast his argument in other terms. He concluded that the Court was overworked largely because of the acceptance of such matters as the F.E.L.A. cases and presented statistics to back up his demand that the situation be remedied. Shortly thereafter, an eminent scholar published an article in the *Harvard Law Journal* which concluded that the Supreme Court was overworked and presented statistics remarkably like those that had been cited by Justice Frankfurter. FF brought the article down to Daddy and said, "You see, Hugo, I am not the only one who feels the Court is overworked."

Daddy smiled. "Felix, don't you think I know where that article came from? Aren't you the same fella been telling us that we ought to follow the English practice where every judge files a separate concurring opinion in every case? You know there is nobody who can honestly say that this Court is overworked now, but not even you could keep up if we followed that English practice."

FF just picked up his papers and left without saying another word to Daddy.

FF served as the literary executor of both Justice Oliver Wendell Holmes and Justice Louis Dembitz Brandeis, and he was considered to be an expert on their philosophies. When hard-pressed, FF was not averse to stating, "Why, what I'm proposing is nothing but an extension of the views of Brandeis," or, "This is nothing more than something Holmes once said to me."

When I was in FF's office one day and he was explaining to me how silly a jury verdict was in an F.E.L.A. case that Daddy wanted to restore, FF was standing by a lectern on which there was a yellow pad. Suddenly, he said to me, "A great Justice like Holmes never once in his career committed an absurdity. Your father is about to commit one here, Hugo. It is a pity because he has been moving toward the status of great." Then FF picked up a pencil and, off on another tack, commented, "You know, I always write standing at a lectern. It stimulates the flow of blood to the head. Learned that from Holmes; that's the way he always wrote."

With all his brilliance, charm and stratagems, however,

FF could not really match Daddy in picking up converts. Even though their passionate conviction of the righteousness of their positions was equal, there was one important difference that gave Hugo the edge. FF had gained his reputation in an academic system, where he was mainly concerned with instructing, not persuading. But Hugo had gotten ahead by convincing ordinary citizens—juries, voters—as well as congressmen and judges, that his view was right. When out to persuade, FF was likely to try to instruct his brethren by presenting an intellectual tour de force, often in language that was more a display of his exceptional vocabulary than a means of communication. FF tended to believe that he was a member of an intellectual elite, and before long some of his colleagues came to believe that FF did not consider them to be of this elite and may have resented his attitude. Hugo, on the other hand, believed in no elite of any kind. If he thought he was brighter than any of the brethren, he never admitted it. Whenever he wished to make a point, he tried to persuade the other Justices with the same simple rhetoric he used with juries and political audiences, employing among other things his sound logic, acting and storytelling abilities, and quotations from great men of the past.

But if Hugo can be considered the leader of any philosophy that finally prevailed over FF's convictions, that came more than anything else from Hugo's flat refusal to acknowledge even to himself that any other Justice ever followed him. In fact, he was apt to become upset when others suggested he was a leader. He was never any angrier than he was one night after a "fool testimonial dinner" in his behalf where the master of ceremonies claimed that Justices Wiley Rutledge and

Frank Murphy followed him. Immediately afterwards he called both Justices and apologized. I heard him say to each, "Good Lord, the guy's got it reversed. You two fellas been leading me around if anybody's been doing any leading." Too frequently for Daddy, an article would come out suggesting that a more accurate description of the "Warren Court" might be the "Black Court." Whenever this would happen, he would exclaim, "Those fellas always been against my views. They're just trying to get the Chief down on me. Nobody can lead the Chief. He is more hard-headed and opinionated than I am."

And I would say, "That's a tall order, Daddy."

Despite all the conflicts between them, FF and Hugo always maintained lively communication, even if sometimes they did argue like boys in a schoolyard. Both were bored by spectator sports, and thought very little of Fred Vinson's and Earl Warren's enthusiasm for such activities. "The Chief has one more sport than Fred," FF commented to Hugo one day. "Or was Fred also a shark on fighting?"

FF loved my mother, and so did Marion, his wife. Mama never entered the courtroom that FF did not drop out of the proceedings for a moment to write the first of many short notes that a messenger would hand Mama one after the other until she left. The notes might say anything from "Welcome. We have needed some sunlight to brighten this dreary day," to "Surely, you cannot have a son that age," to "You could do a much better job on this case than this lawyer." When Mama came into the courtroom, it seemed as if all he thought of was what he was going to say in the next note to her.

FF had no children of his own, and he always displayed

a real interest in all of the Black kids. Indeed, he was not far behind Daddy in giving me advice. Once when he dropped over to the house to chitchat with Daddy sometime after Mama died, we were all enjoying some bourbon when FF admonished me: "Hugo, have you never learned the joys of good conversation while you sip—not gulp— a drink?"

One day when I was at Yale Law School trying to write a law journal paper, I came down to the Court for a little help from Daddy. FF saw me walking down the hall and quickly drew out of me the purpose of my visit. After leading me into his office, he examined my draft and commenced to give me what I had come down to get from Daddy: "Hugo, hasn't anyone ever taught you how to organize a piece of work—" And so it went for about an hour and a half.

After FF had a stroke in 1961, he learned that I had moved from Alabama to Florida. Instinctively, he knew the reasons why. He sent word by Daddy not to worry, that I had something special that would take me to the top of the legal profession wherever I was. Daddy also reported that he added: "This is because he is Josephine's son."

Daddy and FF carried on a lively exchange about their differences in writing opinions. FF claimed that Hugo tended to oversimplify, while Daddy retorted that FF felt this way because of a tendency on his part to overcomplicate. FF fired back, "Simplify—the end of man! A gentleman named Procrustes was for simplicity."

Because of FF's refusal to vote to grant certiorari in F.E.L.A. cases where judges had nullified jury verdicts in favor of workers, Daddy accused FF of not really believ-

ing in jury trials. A friend of them both, Judge Jerome
Frank of the Second Circuit Court of Appeals, had come
out openly with a proposal to abolish juries in F.E.L.A.
cases. Once, FF warned Daddy: "As to hostility to jury,
don't mix up Frankfurter with Frank." Another time
when FF went against his usual policy, he said to Daddy,
"I feel that my work today almost entitles me to a good
word from you. I voted to grant and reverse an F.E.L.A.
assumption of risk case."

When FF first came on the Court, Justice McReynolds
treated him in a barbaric fashion. One can only speculate
why he did this. It is known that McReynolds felt that the
old reactionary Court, then known as "The Nine Old
Men," was too liberal, and in McReynolds' own circle, FF
and the Harvard Law School represented hard-core liberalism. In any event, McReynolds even refused to attend
FF's robing ceremonies. Nevertheless, McReynolds
thereafter occasionally tried to win FF and even Hugo
over to his side. "Hugo," FF would say to Daddy whenever this happened, "McReynolds is in one of his cooing
moods today."

Justice Douglas always pained FF, and I'm sure the
feeling was mutual. In 1951 FF read an article in *Look* by
Douglas, who recommended a political settlement with
China, and took it as a slur on Dean Acheson, one of his
favorite protégés. As did many politicians and Justices, FF
would frequently approach Hugo about the controversial
Justice because Daddy got along with Douglas very well.
This time FF complained, "Dean has tried for a political
settlement. There is no reason to expect Dulles could get
it or Bill Douglas could get it if Dean could not get it."

Many times Daddy and FF ended up defending the

same side of an issue, and on those occasions, FF would plot with Hugo on ways to capture a brother for their side. But sometimes Hugo considered FF's being on his side a mixed blessing. Shortly after Mama died, I was visiting Daddy when FF arrived to pay him a call. FF was his most charming self, recounting anecdotes about Brandeis, Holmes and his days at Harvard as a teacher. Among other things, he remarked, "When I was at Harvard, I told my students, 'If you lose a suit in equity, you may win on the decree.'"

When FF had gone, I said to Daddy, "I thought you showed some special interest in that business about winning on the decree."

"I did, Son. I got to watch Felix like a hawk even when he is supposed to be on the same side with me. Sometimes he tries to stick in language that makes it easy for some judge on the district court or one of the courts of appeals to be able to reject the case as a precedent. I've known it a long time and looked out for it, but his statement about winning on the decree makes me positive what I've suspected is true."

FF rarely had a good word for the lawyers who argued cases before the Supreme Court. He remarked to Hugo during the course of one argument: "Lawyers can and will argue anything." Frequently FF would shoot Daddy a note writing off everything the lawyer was saying with the unflattering comment: "That's lawyer's logic." Another time during the course of an argument, FF passed Daddy a note saying, "Can't you, without encroachment on the First Amendment, gag him?"

There is, of course, a perennial ego conflict between lawyers and judges. Judges are not averse to discovering an issue that the lawyers have missed and then deciding a case on the basis of that point. Frequently, those lawyers who use every possible stratagem to win will plant a clue in a brief on one of several points the case could go off on, in the event that one of the judges is anxious to discover something on his own. When the judge discovers the point and rules for the lawyer, and implies that the lawyer is a fool for basing his brief on the wrong side, the lawyer does not mind. His ego is bruised but the case has been won. One day while I was in Daddy's office, FF burst in afire with enthusiasm: "The lawyer's missed the entire point in this case. This is what it's all about—" And he proceeded to lay it out for Daddy, who also became excited: "You know something, Felix. I think you have really hit on something."

After FF left, Daddy picked up the brief and began to restudy it. Before too long, he handed it to me with his thumb on a spot. "Take a look at this, Son. Do you think these lawyers maybe wanted us to discover this point on our own?"

Quite often during a lawyer's argument FF would preempt his limited time by asking questions in a tone that made the lawyer feel like a fool. In such situations, a lawyer is helpless. Even if he could put the judge down with an appropriate retort, he dares not, because, after all, the judge is a part of the institution the lawyer is trying to persuade. There simply is no contest unless one of the other judges in effect takes the place of the lawyer who is being denied his opportunity to argue. In that event, the contest can become a beautiful thing to behold. Frequently, when FF commenced this kind of questioning, Hugo would interrupt him and begin asking the lawyer a series of leading questions, the premises of which tended to refute the arguments FF was making in the guise of questions. When the session ended, FF and Daddy would sometimes emerge from the robing room into the hall of the Court, still carrying on the argument.

Only rarely did their arguments degenerate into querulousness. If FF stomped out, either he would be back in Daddy's office the next day or Daddy would go to FF's and the argument would continue. Once I remember Daddy laughing and saying after a conference, "I thought Felix was going to hit me today, he got so mad. But he'll get over it." But this sort of thing never really bothered him. "Felix just gets mad quick and gets over it, Son. It doesn't hurt anything."

Although FF always resumed relations with Daddy immediately after one of their sharp encounters, the matter apparently did not leave his mind so soon. Frequently, he would retire to his office and dictate a memorandum or make an angry entry in his diary of his version of the encounter, replete with not-so-complimentary personal comments. Although up until his dying day FF believed he had kept this practice a secret, Hugo soon learned that FF was making these notations to influence history. When Daddy mentioned this to me, I asked him what he was going to do to protect himself.

"Nothing, Son. Felix just gets mad when somebody stands in his way. The stuff is probably like a bunch of letters a fella writes to blow off steam but never mails. If it's more, it will backfire on Felix if he continues and preserves it for history. Making secret memoranda about court business for history reflects a lot more about the character of the author than it does information about the subjects. Felix is both a very smart man and a very good man. He will probably destroy the stuff before he dies." But FF, unfortunately, did not destroy his notes; the material reposes in the Congressional Library for the eyes of historians or anyone else who wishes to see it.

For a while during the time FF was on the Court, there existed what was known in those days as "Black constitutional law professors" and "Frankfurter constitutional law professors." These professors went at it tooth and nail both in law journal articles and at social affairs. The most severe split came between certain Yale and Harvard professors. Very insulting things were said at Yale about FF, and at Harvard about Daddy and Justice Douglas— sometimes on a personal level. All of this sorely distressed Hugo. He urged those who thought they were supporting him to stop arguing on a personal basis about FF, but for a while he had very little success. While I was at Yale Law School, he said to me, "Felix is not a bad fella, and he is not wrong all that much. If the fellas who think they are helping me and Bill will quiet down—who knows what may happen a few years from now. It might be Felix, Bill and me against the others. Please tell those fellas that I want them to stop this feuding around with Felix."

To some extent, this proved prophetic, for Hugo felt that FF was magnificent in the days of the McCarthy hysteria that followed soon after. Although Daddy was very unhappy with the work of the Supreme Court during the McCarthy era, he felt more confidence in FF during those days than in any other single justice except Bill Douglas. "Without Felix to help Bill and me in those days, I am not at all sure that the Court might not have lent real

aid and comfort to McCarthy and like-minded nuts instead of timidly slapping 'em on the wrists now and then.
Felix shared the mistrust and contempt that Bill and I
have for informers, and Felix shared the feeling that Bill
and I have that the First Amendment prevents government from getting after a man directly or indirectly because of his speech, no matter how wild it is.''

There were only two matters concerning FF that ever
really bothered Hugo. The first was the idea FF launched
through his network of protégés in academic circles that
Daddy had become a judicial activist, that Hugo Black
stood ready at any minute to knock down any legislative
act on the basis of his notions of right and wrong, regard-
less of the Constitution. This was a totally unjust criticism. Daddy remembered what had happened when the
Nine Old Men had followed their own notions of right
and wrong, and distrusting the Constitution, had struck
down every piece of social legislation passed by Congress
or state legislatures. He was not about to subject himself
to the same criticisms he and the others had leveled at
those Justices. "Even though legislation is cockeyed and
thoroughly unwise, it's not the Court's function to strike
it down for that reason, openly or disguisedly. Actually,
Felix and his people are much more likely to rule on their
notion of right and wrong than I am. Whereas I say the
due process clause of the Fourteenth Amendment in-
cludes the first ten amendments to the Constitution and
test state laws that way, Felix and his people claim the
right to knock down anything under that due process
clause that 'shocks the judicial conscience.' What in the
world is that but testing a law on the judges' notions of
right and wrong? It just allows a fella who wants to do

what he thinks is right to shoot the works."

The other thing that FF and his protégés did that really got under Daddy's skin was the articles they published faulting his research and historical conclusions. He bitterly resented the charges that he had consciously and in bad faith distorted history to his own purposes. "Son, I am perfectly satisfied that my history in those opinions is right. And I feel that those fellas are too, or they would not sink to that personal level." I am not prepared to defend my father's versions of history, because I am no authority and have not done the work he did on it. But one thing I do know. He was convinced that what he had done was right, and he never used a version that he believed was in any way inaccurate simply to give weight to his own argument.

Despite these two sore points, Hugo and FF carried on a meaningful dialogue right up to the day FF died: either FF would burst into Daddy's office or Hugo would say, "I think I'll ease down to Felix's." When FF finally had to retire for his health many years before Hugo's time came, the communication between the two remained vigorously intact. FF, even though afflicted, retained a lively interest in Court business, writing Daddy notes and letters and calling him on the telephone in an effort to get him to vote as FF would have voted. Although FF could not get out of his car, he would have his messenger drive him out to our house on South Lee Street, and Daddy would come out and get in the back seat with FF where he would receive advice. "Plenty of it good too, Son," Daddy would report afterwards.

On the day that I learned of FF's retirement, I sat down and wrote him a letter, telling him that I thought the running debate between him and my father may have been the most constructive thing that happened in this country during the years they served together. Once they finished one of their exchanges, the probabilities that the Supreme Court would do the right thing were greatly increased; it was highly unlikely that the brethren had not been exposed to everything that could be said about both sides of a particular case. Daddy has a book of FF's papers inscribed by FF: "For Hugo Black, whose fault it won't be if my mental veins harden."

Bill
Douglas

If any student of the modern Supreme Court took an association test, the word "Black" would probably evoke the response "Douglas" and vice versa. For more than thirty years, the two sat together, and the odds are that in any given case, even toward the end of Daddy's career, the two would have voted together.

Daddy sometimes reacted to criticism of Justice Douglas with the same intensity he might have to criticism of himself if he had ever let himself go. Justice Frankfurter knew this. So one day, being very agitated about Douglas's conduct in a certain instance—behavior which FF considered inconsistent with "a civilized concept of judicial dignity"—he cleverly veiled his criticism of Justice Douglas to Daddy in a flattering remark: "A great Justice must be an austere puritan as you are, Hugo."

"Let him who is without sin cast the first stone," Daddy replied.

Bill Douglas is a loner, a man with an artistic temperament, unwilling or unable to yield any of his personal freedom to the restraints of conventional society. Such a person functions best as a great creative person when he can perform alone. But when he is required to work with others, he will be lost without a sympathetic person within his particular field of activity. For most of their service together, Hugo acted as the liaison between Bill Douglas and the Court, and this function must be considered one of Daddy's important contributions to his country; talent like Bill Douglas's should not be allowed to go to waste.

Douglas is a person who simply refuses to fit in; he is profoundly anti-establishment. He loves his perpetual status as a rebel, and he has preferred to spend most of his life as the unpredictable and obstinate loner. As an epigraph to his book *Go East, Young Man,* he quoted from Jalal ud-din Rumi, Persian poet (1207–1293): "All your anxiety is because of your desire for harmony. Seek disharmony; then you will gain peace." Justice Douglas disturbs people, may even offend them, and but for Daddy's love for him, might not have been able to contribute as meaningfully as he has to the Court. I believe that my father's efforts helped to make his gifts effective on the Court; he has been a constant source of vital unrest and a spur to bold, intrepid ideas.

Hugo felt a unique bond with Bill Douglas and always maintained a special kinship with him. Daddy had to do the giving in the department of ego, pride and dignity to keep the relationship viable, but he felt it was worth it to him and to the country. "The fella is a genius, Son, and he's got right instincts on social and political issues. Of course, nobody's perfect—but me," he would add with a wink.

Like Daddy, Bill Douglas traveled a long way to his seat on the Supreme Court. Coming from a humble background in Washington State, he worked his way through Columbia Law School and then put in a stint with a Wall Street law firm. Later he went on to teach at Columbia and then at Yale Law School, where Dean Robert Hutchins had assembled a most remarkable faculty, including Thurman Arnold and Wesley Sturges. From there he was appointed to the Securities and Exchange Commission, which he soon chaired, all the while carrying out his investigations of corruption with the utmost integrity. During this time he once wrote my father and congratulated him on his lone dissent holding that a corporation was not a person within the due process clause. In 1939 he was appointed to the Court.

Bill Douglas is a ruggedly handsome man, his distinctive feature being a shock of hair with a lock that falls over his forehead and a cowlick in back. While he is talking in his soft, Western brogue, he is likely to dart his hand to his head or to pull his ear violently, movements which hint of a vast store of nervous energy.

The public always confused Hugo with Justice Douglas. Once on behalf of a wronged wife, I took on a divorce case involving a middle-aged pilot who had run off with a young stewardess. As I pressed him on cross-examination, the man jumped up and pointed an indignant finger at me, saying, "You got a lot of nerve jumping up and down about me, after all the young women your father has chased after." I coolly told him he had my father mixed up with someone else.

Despite these differences in life-style, if Hugo could not announce an opinion, he would ask Justice Douglas to do it for him, and vice versa. Daddy used to laugh and say, "The time I thought Bill was consistently more sound than any other period during our service together was the time when he fell off the mountain and cracked himself up real bad. He was in the hospital for several months out in Arizona, and I virtually had his proxy." They always carried on a lively communication, passing notes to each other as well as visiting in each other's office. Once in the early 1940's, Douglas wrote a note in connection with the proclivity of the old Court to shoot down social legislation because it violated the due process clause: "No patent medicine was ever put to wider and more varied use than the Fourteenth Amendment." Daddy really enjoyed that one.

Shortly after the election of Richard Nixon in 1968, Daddy was contacted by the executive branch about possible impeachment of Justice Douglas. Hugo responded without any hesitation: "Bill shouldn't be impeached. He has been imprudent sometimes, but he has never ruled from a corrupt motive. Sure, he has sometimes ruled out of prejudice. He'll always vote for a labor union, because he thinks government has got to sponsor power to countervail against privilege. But Bill is honest—and he cannot be blackmailed. He doesn't see anything wrong with his personal life. I tell you this. If they try to impeach Bill, I'll offer him my services. I've got one more hard trial in me. If they impeach, they'll do it just because he is champion of the weak against the strong, and that's just wrong. I believe we could whip 'em good."

Hugo always had a special kinship with Justices Douglas, Frank Murphy, Wiley Rutledge, Earl Warren, William

Brennan, Arthur Goldberg and Thurgood Marshall, Justices who believed that the underprivileged should be protected.

He used to say, "Smartest thing these reactionaries ever did from their point of view was to shunt the Chief off onto this Court. Not that he has not been great here. But the Chief could have gone all the way. He's one of the greatest vote-getters ever. What a President he would have made. They could never have gotten him out—anti-third term statute and all—until he was ready to go."

Going by a code of social morality, Daddy would probably have agreed with these Justices on any particular case. But all of these men troubled him, although not in the same way as a John Marshall or a James Clark McReynolds, two of his symbols of reactionary conservatism, did. He would say, "The Chief, Brennan, Bill Douglas, Arthur, Thurgood, are usually going to do the right thing. Sometimes they're too gullible, but they always mean well. They're kind of like Marcus Aurelius. While they're around, we'll generally get just judgment. But when they're gone and we get a McReynolds type, he's free to let go with his bad sense of right and wrong. I believe we've got to tie the judges of this Court and the subordinate federal courts to something lasting, even if we've got to sacrifice doing some good through the federal courts. We don't want this Court to get to be like one of these agencies—one law when the Republicans are in and another when the Democrats are in. This Court's got to have some enduring principles."

It was this concern that bothered him most in the days of the Warren Court. He feared that these excellent men sometimes carried their sense of right and wrong so far that a reaction might set in, giving their enemies issues like "law and order" and "strict construction" to exploit. Daddy had crusaded for the principle that black people should receive privileges equal to whites', but no greater; and he felt strongly that disorder should not be tolerated even in the interest of justice. It frustrated him that he could not make them see the necessity of finding enduring principles that would prohibit even a John Marshall from reconverting the Court to a fortress of the mighty. "And, Son, I've got so little time," he would say to me when discussing this matter.

"Daddy," I said, "haven't you ever considered Justice Douglas and those fellas may be right?"

"They're wrong. No doubt about it. We are putting our heads on the block for our enemies to chop off. There is going to be a reaction, and this country will be lucky to survive it."

Since he wasn't always able to persuade the Warren Court to listen to his views, he went on television for a series of programs in an attempt to forestall any extreme reaction to the Court's rulings. He wanted the people of America to see in person the man who had been cast as a symbol of the big bad liberal Supreme Court; the man who was falsely accused of encouraging disorder on the streets and the boldness of rapists. He wanted Americans to see that this man bore a strong resemblance to the ordinary man and shared the same fears and hopes.

Nevertheless, the reaction came. Nixon won in 1968 on the issues of law and order and strict construction. At that time Daddy commented to me: "That fella knows nothing about real law or order. He only knows about the kind of law and order it takes to protect and enlarge the property of special privilege. 'Strict construction' to him just means construction for privilege. But the people would rather have imbalance in privilege and the right to walk securely on the streets than no privilege and fear on the streets. He and his bunch are bad fellas. I am not sure this country can survive them. And the tragedy is, these truly great and good men like the Chief and Bill made it easier for 'em —out of the purest motives—by permitting these bullies to terrorize the streets in the name of just causes. And, Son, I couldn't stop 'em. If I had been younger, well— Maybe the next time after this when we get the Court— maybe, maybe—the new generation will realize that the sanctuary must be built on absolutes if it is to endure."

The
Letter

In July of 1971, about a month after the Supreme Court ruled that the newspapers could continue publishing the Pentagon Papers, I had a call from Elizabeth. She told me that my father, then eighty-five years old, had written a letter to my brother Sterling's daughter, Ann, in which he virtually announced he was dying. I also learned that he had developed headaches which as yet were undiagnosed.

In the middle of that month I flew up to Washington on a business trip, and immediately went to call on him. Daddy at first took up the condition of Elizabeth's mother, who was suffering from cancer: "Mrs. Seay is finished. I am worried. I want to go to her funeral, but I know I can't. I want the family to be represented there."

"Daddy," I said, "you know I'll go if you want me to."

"What if you have a trial?"

"If I do, Daddy, I'll just have to walk out of it with a mistrial, or whatever. If you want me to be there, I will."

He said nothing else for a while, but he was clearly working up to say something, and I kept still. Finally:

"Son, you know Elizabeth's got the same problem with me she's got with her mother."

I pretended not to hear.

"Daddy, what do the doctors say these headaches are?"

"Trouble is, they don't know, Son, but I do—"

I avoided that too and said, "Daddy, I've got a hard day tomorrow. Would you mind if I went to bed?"

"All right, but remember, Son, if anything happens—"

"Remember what?"

"Go to Mrs. Seay's funeral. You are the head of the family. Protect everything just like I was there."

I rubbed his head. "I'll do the best I can, Daddy, but I'm not you—you'll be there yourself."

He gave me a grin and shook his head. "Face reality, Son."

"I am," I said, then I blew him a kiss and went to bed.

But, as usual, he knew things I did not. In the middle of August I got a long-distance call from my sister Jo-Jo: "Hugo, Daddy has given up. He has just quit. He is convinced he is going to die. You have got to go up there."

As soon as I hung up, I called Elizabeth and Daddy. Elizabeth answered. "Hugo," she said, "I will go to the other phone and put your Daddy on this one. He wants to talk to you and so do I."

His voice sounded the same as always to me—very strong and youthful. "Son, are you there?"

"Yeah," I said.

Elizabeth broke in: "Hugo, your Daddy has written his retirement message. He says he can't see and says he has got to quit. His health has deteriorated. He has wasted away down to a hundred and fifteen pounds. He won't eat. He wants you to come up tomorrow."

It was the middle of the week and I had lots to do. "Can we wait till the weekend?" I asked.

"No," he replied, "unless you want me to send in the letter before you see it. I can't wait, Son. The time has come."

"Can you do it, Hugo?" Elizabeth said.

I answered, "I will be there just as soon as I can get a plane."

Elizabeth started to cry softly. From the other phone Daddy said, "You got a cold, Elizabeth?"

"All right, folks," I said. "I will see you tomorrow."

I hung up, then, and wept.

Before I flew up to Washington from Miami I tried to figure out if there was something I could use to help change his solemn belief that he was finished. As I browsed through my library I came across Cicero's essay "On Old Age." Maybe this would inspire him by reminding him that the great affairs of life are not performed by physical strength or nimbleness of body, but by deliberation, character and wise counsel—qualities that Daddy surely had even in his eighty-fifth year.

When I arrived in Washington it was midafternoon. Daddy was fully dressed, but acted peculiarly.

"Son," he said, "I can't do my job, 'cause I can't see. I've got to quit. Here, I've written this."

He handed me a letter to President Nixon. "Lou Oberdorfer [one of Daddy's law clerks] and I wrote it," he said. "I always told you I would know when I had to get off the Court—and the time has come."

I finished reading and said, "What do the doctors say?"

"They are not sure yet, but I am. I know. I just can't see with this stuff I got."

"What stuff?" I said.

"This temporal arteritis, Son."

"They've diagnosed it?"

"Yeah. And you know what Orlando died of, obliterative—get this—arteritis."

"Well, they aren't the same thing," I said.

"How do you know? They're very close. You don't know anything about it."

"What's this got to do with seeing?" I asked.

"Plenty, and I'll tell you something else. John Harlan can't see a thing. He ought to get off the Court too."

"Daddy, let that be the last time you talk like that. That's none of your business. How many times you tell me never to say something like that. Good Lord."

"You're right, Son. I am tired. I'm going to take off my clothes and take a little nap."

Elizabeth fixed some dinner and then sent me upstairs to wake Daddy. As was my habit, I leaped up the stairs two at a time, whistling all the way. Before I could get into the room, I heard him fussing at me. "Son, what do you mean, whistling like that when I'm in this desperate condition."

"Daddy," I said, "I apologize. I just came up to get you for supper."

"I don't feel like going down there, Son."

"Okay, I'll bring it to you up here, Daddy."

"Well, I won't eat it," he said.

I brought the food to him and made him sit up. When he would not lift the fork, I went over, picked up some food and smiled at him.

"Open up," I said. "Remember those words?"

He did open up but, after about five bites, he said, "That's about it, isn't it, Son?"

"No," I said, "you need more."

"Take it away, I don't."

That night the doctors instructed Elizabeth to take him to Bethesda Naval Hospital the next day. Although he did not want to go, he seemed to resign himself to it. That evening I still figured everything would turn out all right. He still seemed clear-minded and strong-voiced, and he had not insisted I send out the retirement letter.

The next day I drove him and Elizabeth out to the hospital in the pouring rain. When we arrived he was too weak to get out of the car and we had to use a wheelchair. He was assigned to a private room in the VIP Tower next to Justice John Harlan, who had been there two weeks suffering from back pains that the doctors could not diagnose. Although Justice Harlan had always been considered a conservative, he and Daddy had been very close personal friends from the time Justice Harlan first came on the bench almost twenty years after Daddy had taken his seat. They even claimed to be related to each other through some Harlans back in Hugo's mother's family line.

Practically the first thing Daddy wanted me to do once he was installed in the hospital was to go out and burn certain papers of his. According to him, publishing the notes of conversations between Justices inhibited the free exchange of ideas. "You remember how you told me that a tape recorder always chilled any real negotiation in a labor dispute, Son, with everybody spending all their time making a record?" he said. "What I'm talking about is the same kind of thing." He also felt that reports by one Justice of another's conduct in the heat of a difference might unfairly and inaccurately reflect history. As an example, he cited to me a biographer's accusation, based on Justice Harold Burton's papers, alleging that Daddy had hung back on the decision ending segregation of the races. "Good Lord, Son, you of all people know how false that is."

When he requested me to burn the papers, I tried to put it off, since I did not think this should be done. "You'll have plenty of time when you retire to do it yourself. You know the ones you want to keep and the ones you want to destroy."

"I want you to do it. There isn't time for me."

Then he changed the subject.

"Son," he said, "I want you to send Spencer over to the White House with my retirement letter right now. Then deliver it to each of the judges in the building, including the retired ones."

I had dreaded this. The doctors had told me and Elizabeth not to let him send the letter because they still felt he might recover his strength. But he insisted, "They don't know what they're talking about. I'm finished, Son. I want that thing sent before it happens."

I took a different tack. "Daddy, you don't want to send that thing before I get those papers out of there and burn them. I might not be able to get the same cooperation I can while you have the full power of your office as senior judge."

He thought for a minute. "You're right, Son. We'll hold up until you get them burned. But get right on it."

Shortly after this conversation Elizabeth and I asked Lou Oberdorfer to draw up a letter authorizing me to destroy any papers selected "in my discretion." When we presented it to Daddy, he took it from Elizabeth and read it carefully. "Good Lord," he exclaimed from his bed. "Give me a pen. Can't anybody do anything right?" Carefully placing a comma after the word "discretion," he then wrote in a strong hand: "so long as he destroys them all."

Dealing with his papers was not the only problem I had at this time. As soon as he entered the hospital, newsmen besieged the hospital public relations department for reports on his condition. Elizabeth and I felt that the hospital should be free to give a report, but Daddy disagreed.

"Tell them nothing," he said.

"What about your clerks and members of the court?"

"Tell them nothing too."

"Daddy—"

"Son, it's my life, isn't it?"

"Yes."

"Then do as I say."

He wanted to see no one. Whoever it might be who asked to visit, he would say, "I can't do anything for him and he can't do anything for me." Once he agreed to see the Chief Justice, but it was a short visit during which Elizabeth and I were not allowed to talk.

At first, Elizabeth and I and the doctors believed that if we could chase out of his mind the idea that he was "finished," his strength would return. Although he fussed very little about it, we felt he begrudged the time Elizabeth spent attending her mother, who was in her nineties. So I told him that Elizabeth had made up her mind to put her mother in a nursing home as soon as Daddy left the hospital. But this didn't cheer him up. He simply commented, "I knew about that problem when I married her."

One day I brought him several treatises on temporal arteritis that I had gotten from a medical library, and read to him statements that this disease was neither fatal nor permanently disabling. But he just shrugged and said, "Did you read anything about the stuff in a man my age?"

"Yes," and I read this to him, but he refused to believe what he heard. When that didn't work I tried reading Cicero's "On Old Age" to him, but he spurned it, saying, "That's for healthy old men. Not men in the desperate condition I am in."

Not long after this the nurse told me of a conversation she had with him. When she tried to convince him he would recover, he replied, "If I were not in a very desperate condition my son Hugo wouldn't stay up here. Nothing but that could keep him away from his work."

A couple of days later I walked up to Daddy and said, "Well, Daddy, I'm going home. The doctors say you are going to go home in two or three days, and I've got work to do."

"They're wrong, Son. They're wrong. I am not going to go home again."

"Well, Daddy, I've got to believe them. You'll go home if you want to."

"Son, I want to. I'm trying, I'm trying."

"Well, I can come back up if the doctors are wrong."

"It may be too late, Son."

"Well—" I hung my head.

"Now," he said, "you aren't going anywhere."

And I did not.

The last thing I tried on him was a tactic he might have used on me. One afternoon I told him, "Daddy, I've always been proud of you—always. But for the first time I'm a little ashamed."

"Ashamed," he said heatedly. "Ashamed of what?"

"You have quit, Daddy, you aren't even trying. And I've bragged to these doctors you don't know what it is to quit. I told them you would fight to live harder than anybody they ever saw. And you have just quit."

"I have not," he yelled back at me. "I have not. What you want me to do?"

"I want you to get off your duff and walk around this place and try to get some strength. Lying up in that bed drains you."

"All right. All right—I'll try."

At that moment Elizabeth came into the room. "He wants you to walk up and down the hall with him, Elizabeth," I said.

I went outside and met Justice Harlan, who was leaning against the wall smoking. All of a sudden Daddy and Elizabeth emerged from the room, arm in arm, Daddy almost going at the "All Policemen Have Big Feet" pace. Suddenly, without looking to the side, he sniffed and said, "John, you're smokin'," and kept on staring forward. My eyes met Justice Harlan's and I smiled. It was a beautiful moment.

Every day he would ask me for a report on the destruction of the papers until I finally realized I could put it off no longer. It wouldn't have been possible for me to have done this burning if I hadn't been absolutely sure that this was not simply my father's spur-of-the-moment decision.

Fifteen years ago he had made it clear to me exactly what papers he wanted destroyed, and he let me know in no uncertain terms that it would be my job to dispose of them if he was unable to do it himself. Also, he assured me that certain friends of his, law professors, had letters from him describing his intentions.

With the help of Frances Lamb, his secretary, I collected his notes at the Supreme Court Building and took them to South Lee Street. There in the back room, I sat down for a while and slowly leafed through them, fascinated by my father's compact, pregnant summaries of the attitudes and comments of each Justice. Then I forced myself to throw them in the fire I had built in the fireplace. In the beginning, it wasn't just the smoke that made my eyes fill with tears. When I would leave for the hospital, Spencer would continue the burning.

After several days of this, the Pollution Department of Alexandria called and asked us to stop the burning. Neighbors had complained not only of the smoke but of flying bits of charred paper everywhere in the air. We relocated at the home of Elizabeth's son, Fred DeMeritte, out in Maryland. There Jo-Jo, Fred and his children and I recommenced the burning ceremonies.

Occasionally, Daddy would bear down on me about finishing and fuss at me, "You got to hurry, Son. I can't do my job and I want that letter to go in." But I was not about to finish and thereby set the stage for sending the retirement letter until the doctors told me that all hope for return to normal was gone.

After a week or so, Jo-Jo came up from her home in Hackensack to join me and Elizabeth at the hospital. There was not really much we could do for him, since he had no interest in television, radio, newspapers, games, books or conversation.

The worst job, however, fell to Elizabeth. She was the principal feeder in those dreadful last days. No child ever balked more at eating than he did then, and often he was positively nasty. I got so disgusted with him, I said, "Elizabeth is trying her level best to save your life and all you're doing is grumbling and growling around like an old bear."

"I am not," he replied harshly. But when Elizabeth came back in, he said, looking adoringly at her, "You're mighty sweet."

Sometimes while I was sitting in the room with him, I would notice him looking at his hands; first he would move all the fingers, then one at a time, then a single joint.

"What are you doing, Daddy?"

"Just checkin' to see if a stroke has hit me."

Justice
John Marshall Harlan
at Sunset

At the hospital, Elizabeth and I tried as much as we could to be helpful to Justice Harlan, who was next door to Daddy. His wife was in a nursing home, while his daughter in Connecticut found it impossible to get away from her five children. Since Elizabeth and I spent almost every day at the hospital, we were able to spend a good deal of time with him. The intimate relationship that developed between seventy-four-year-old Justice Harlan and me during this darkest hour of my life is one of the most treasured I have ever had with anyone. Even though he suffered excruciating pain in his back, was losing his sight, and no doubt was haunted by thoughts of imminent death, he possessed a wonderful sense of humor.

Every afternoon just before supper, Justice Harlan and I would enjoy a cocktail hour in his room. Although he had been raised in the Chicago area, he loved the traditions of the South, and always had on hand a bourbon called Rebel Yell. Much of the talk revolved around my father. Did I think Daddy ever aspired to be President?

Did I think Daddy really wanted the longevity record? Did I think Daddy would retire? One day he said, "The biggest difference between your father on the one hand, and me and Justice Frankfurter on the other hand, is the basic assumption we make about judges. Your father believes that you have to keep judges tethered—you can't trust their consciences loose without some kind of bridle."

During those days Justice Harlan still functioned in his job, constantly making and receiving telephone calls to judges, clerks, law students and friends. Unlike Daddy, he loved company and made himself agreeable to everyone. He was sincerely concerned about Daddy's condition and his inability to communicate with him. Since the Bethesda doctors had still not been able to diagnose Harlan's condition, he sought some reassurance from Daddy, but Daddy would not enter into any discussion. I could surmise from the way Justice Harlan acted that in the past Hugo had been able to make him feel certain in areas where he was unsure, and that he sorely missed this right now when he needed it most.

Justice Harlan wanted so much to be able to laugh with Daddy again, and would go into Daddy's room and try to strike up a conversation. One morning he had a petition for certiorari in which the petitioner wanted the Court to declare unconstitutional a certain state law on the ground that in violation of the Fourteenth Amendment, it deprived the petitioner of his property without due process of law. In the past Hugo had chided Justice Harlan for basing his judgment in similar instances upon whether the action "shocked the conscience of the Court," saying that test just allowed Justice Harlan to knock out any law he wished. "The way you interpret that thing, John," Daddy had said, "it's nothing in the world but a shoot-the-works clause." So the morning when Justice Harlan walked in holding this petition he said to Daddy, "Hugo, listen to this. Here's a real candidate for the shoot-the-works clause." Justice Harlan was visibly disappointed when Daddy did not even respond.

The September days wore on and Daddy did not improve. Pressure mounted on me and Elizabeth from the hospital's public relations people for a statement about his condition, but Daddy still wouldn't permit us to say anything, and we had to continue to keep visitors away from him. As if that were not enough, Elizabeth's mother took a turn for the worse and caused her great anxiety.

Although we continued to make Daddy eat and walk about, he was still losing weight. The doctors then told us that the only chance for a cure would be to increase the prednisone dosage, although this would heighten the chance for a stroke. We told them to go ahead, but the increased dosage did not appear to do anything for him. He still did not want to eat or move about, and he became more sensitive to touch and increasingly uncomfortable. The endless blood tests were now real torture for him: "The stuff can't change that often. Please stop them, Son, please."

One day, against his protests as usual, Elizabeth and I walked him out to what we called the "sleeping porch." When we sat down to rest, he seemed preoccupied. Suddenly he looked up and said, "Look there," and he made a circle with his finger. "The eternal cycle," he said, "I'm in its grip."

He noticed the light that blinked when a floor number

is flashed for "heroic measures" for a person "in extremis" and said, "Look at them," making a circle with his finger. I immediately reported this to the doctors. After testing and interviewing him, they told me, "Hugo, he may get well. But we do not think he will return to the physical condition he was in before he was stricken with temporal arteritis."

Meanwhile, I learned that Justice Harlan wanted to see me alone. When I got to his room, I shut the door behind me and said, "What is it, Mr. Justice?"

"Did you lock the door, Hugo?"

"No, sir. But I will." I did this, then said, "What's the matter, Mr. Justice?"

"Hugo," he said, "I need to know about your father's retirement. What is he going to do?"

"Mr. Justice, I think he will retire very soon. Why do you ask right now?"

"I cannot do my job any longer; I believe I have cancer of the spine and I am going to have to retire." Tears ran down his cheeks as he continued, "But I do not want to do anything to detract from the attention your father's retirement will get. I don't have to tell you. He is one of the all-time greats of our Court. He has served with over one-third of the Justices who ever sat on the Court. Nobody's judgment ever exceeded his—his is just the best."

"Mr. Justice," I said, "you must do what you have to do. There will be time."

"Holding up until your father's retirement is recognized and commented on is the right thing to do," he said.

Now he had brought tears to my eyes. "Mr. Justice," I

said, "this is about as noble an act of friendship as there could be. I hate to say this, but I'm not even sure he would do the same thing for you."

"I think he would. But, really, it makes no difference, Hugo," he said. "I would wait anyhow out of respect for his greatness even if he were not my friend."

A few days before this talk, a piece of Justice Harlan's spine had been removed for analysis. The operation went well, but they did it on a Friday, and so he had to wait over the weekend to discover from the analysis whether he would live or die.

On Monday the doctors reported that the specimen for analysis had been lost, and that they would have to take another after he had had a chance to rest. But, in any event, this gentle man became infuriated. He said, "Hugo, we fired a man in our firm who made a mistake of this magnitude. I am going to leave and go to the George Washington Hospital."

"Mr. Justice, I think you are making a mistake. The physical accommodations over there will be less attractive and more expensive. You can't get the attention you get here. Elizabeth, Jo-Jo and I won't be there, since we've got to stay here with Daddy."

"Yes, but at least there won't be another mistake like this."

"Mr. Justice, doctors make mistakes no matter where they are. All hospitals make mistakes."

"You don't want me to go, do you, Hugo?"

"No, sir, I'll miss you too much, and I don't think it's the best thing for you," I said.

"Does your father still have confidence in these doctors?"

"He doesn't have confidence in any doctors, Mr. Justice, except as guessers."

"Well—" Then he decided to try one last time to talk to Daddy, but again Daddy could not respond. Turning to me with tears in his eyes, Justice Harlan said, "Hugo, what is he doing when he circles his finger and points to the ceiling and says 'See 'em. They're coming after me'?"

"Mr. Justice," I said, "did you ever hear him sing 'Swing low sweet chariot, comin' for to carry me home—a band of angels coming after me'?"

"Is he going to die, Hugo?"

"Yes."

"Soon?"

"I'm afraid so. Yes, sir. He has made his mind up, and he is as stubborn and bull-headed about that as everything else."

The next day Justice Harlan moved over to George Washington Hospital. As he sat in his wheelchair in the elevator for his last trip down, my eyes caught his. I felt that he wanted to be taken back to his room, but the doors closed and he was gone.

Hugo
Retires

Justice Harlan had barely left before the doctors cornered me again. One of them said, "Your father's condition just defies us. There is no physical reason why he should continue to deteriorate, but he is. It's almost like the case of an aborigine who was in excellent health, but entered the hospital convinced he was going to die because someone had put a voodoo spell on him. And despite everything, he died."

"You don't think he'll ever recover, then?"

"No."

That night after supper, Daddy seemed bright-eyed and clear-headed. "Daddy," I said, "I've finished burning the papers and I've talked to the doctors. I think probably it's time to let that letter go."

He looked stricken, but all he said was, "All right, Son. I can't do my job. I guess it's time to send it."

That night Elizabeth typed up a duplicate of the letter with a new date, September 14, 1971, on it, and in the morning we presented it to him for signature. Before he signed it, however, he studied it over carefully, even though we told him it was exactly the same as the previous one. "All right," he said, "find me a pen," and he boldly scribbled his signature on it.

When we suggested that the public be given a report on his condition, he smiled at us and said, "They won't care when you let that thing go," referring to the letter of retirement. But, of course, he was wrong. The media pressured the public relations people at the hospital unmercifully after the White House released news of his retirement. We had to give in and allow frequent bulletins about his condition even though we knew he wanted it otherwise. It was the first time I ever consciously acted contrary to his wishes about a matter so personal to him as his own physical condition, and I felt very guilty.

Once I asked him if he'd like to watch the news on television, even though this could cause me trouble because he would hear references to his current condition. But he refused. Neither would he let Elizabeth or me read him the articles in the Washington *Post* and *Star*. "I told you both I don't want to hear that stuff," he said peremptorily.

It seemed almost impossible to cheer him up. One day I said, "Like I've always told you, Daddy, I called you a superstar because of your career, not your tennis." He fired back: "I'll tell you something, Son. If I could see, I could exercise. And if I could exercise, I could have ten more good years and wouldn't be in this desperate condition."

"You can still have those ten good years, Daddy, if you'll try."

He just looked at me and grinned, as if to say, You fool.

The second morning after his retirement they called Elizabeth and me and told us that he had suffered a stroke. When I got out to his room at the hospital, I felt for the first time with all my being that my daddy, as I knew him, was indeed finished. When I remembered the magnificent person he had been, and looked at what I now saw on the hospital bed, I knew that if the luck that had always held for both of us continued, he would die soon. Thinking this made me feel ashamed, and guilty, since I was not altogether certain that I wasn't just worried about all the trouble and inconvenience he would cause me if he survived as an invalid. But whatever it was, I knew I wanted him now to be gone.

At first, Elizabeth, Jo-Jo and I could translate what he said, just as the mother or father of a small child can interpret his gibberish. Then after Daddy suffered another stroke, all he could do was moan.

Yet another stroke hit him a few days hours later. The moaning stopped, his pulse dropped, and he began gasping for breath.

The President inquired about a visit but this was out of the question. Phone calls came from important people from all over the country. We were especially pleased by a resolution from the Alabama state legislature which I read to him, even though now he didn't respond when I talked: ". . . as Justice Black steps down from the bench for a well-deserved rest, the people of Alabama, through their legislature, pray that Providence will ever guide and sustain him, confident that history will regard Justice Black as one of the true giants of jurisprudence . . ."

That night Elizabeth, Jo-Jo and I decided to remain at

the hospital. At about midnight on September 26, 1971, I was awakened by the officer of the day, who said to me, "Mr. Black, Mr. Black, the Justice has passed."

I ran to Daddy's room, and found him lying there, his left eye cocked open. I shut it as tears welled up in my eyes.

Elizabeth, Jo-Jo and I gathered up his stuff, and then Jo-Jo went back into his room and kissed the top of his head.

My father never did like pomp and ceremony in a funeral. "What in the world do they think they're accomplishing for this democracy always leading that saddled white horse without a rider in a funeral parade. That's just the government telling the public we're led by men on white horses. That's dangerous stuff."

We in the family honored his feeling about funerals by choosing a plain pine casket for him. Instead of the ceremonious music of state funerals, the ladies of the family selected his favorite Clay County hymns. All during his days on the Court, Daddy had carried around in his coat pocket for ready reference several little copies of the Constitution which the Government Printing Office sold for ten cents. We laid him to rest with several of these in his suit pocket.

Index

Acheson, Dean, 231
Aeschylus, 157
Alabama *Journal*, 215–16
Alabama Supreme Court, 31, 46
"All Policemen Have Big Feet" (song), 113, 186
Ancient Law (Maine), 53
Aristotle, 120, 134, 137
Arlington Cemetery, 179
Army Air Force, 185
Arnold, Thurman, 71–72, 241
Arnold, Mrs. Thurman, 71
Ashland College, 9

Bankhead, John, 60, 61
Bethesda Naval Hospital, 250, 258
Beveridge, Albert, 158
Birmingham, Ala., 17–26, 27–31, 37, 44–46, 60, 149, 206–17

Birmingham Auditorium, 211
Birmingham Law Library, 51
Birmingham Medical School, 16
Black, Ann, 246
Black, Columbus, 4
Black, Daisy, 15
Black, Elizabeth Graham, 153
Black, Hollis, 100
Black, Mrs. Hugo (Elizabeth DeMeritte), 124, 202–5, 219, 246–52, 254, 255–56, 257, 259, 261, 263–65, 266
Black, Mrs. Hugo (Josephine Foster), 37–41, 42, 43, 63, 64–66, 68, 70, 72, 73, 77–80, 86, 89, 90, 92, 94–96, 102–4, 106, 107, 110, 111, 113, 116, 119, 124, 127, 129–31, 162–63, 167–71, 172, 173, 177–80, 193, 204, 225, 229, 230, 232

Black, Mrs. Hugo, Jr. (Graham Hobson), 129–31, 132, 149, 153, 177, 179, 204
Black, Hugo, III, 153
Black, John Densler, 13, 111
Black, Jo-Jo, 109, 111, 113, 124, 158, 179, 247, 255, 261, 265, 266
Black, Lee, 5, 127
Black, Leon D., Jr., 221, 222
Black, Lucylle, 127–28
Black, Margaret Hartley, 153
Black, Martha Ardella Tolland "Della," 3–4, 5, 10, 11, 15, 16–17
Black, Ora, 9, 81–82
Black, Orlando, 5, 6, 13, 16, 111, 249
Black, Pelham, 5–6
Black, Sterling, 13, 41, 42, 61, 76, 91, 92, 93, 102, 108, 112, 113, 124, 126, 164, 172, 178, 179, 246
Black, Vernon, 5
Black, William Lafayette "Fate," 3–5, 6, 9, 12, 13, 16–17
Black-Connery bill, 87–88
Blackmun, Harry, 148
Blanshard, Paul, 104
Bradford, Col. Bob, 203
Bramble Bush (Llewellyn), 119
Brandeis, Louis Dembitz, 145, 195, 223, 227, 232
Brennan, William, 242–43
Brown v. Board of Education, 191, 208–9
Bryan, William Jennings, 32

Burns, Robert, 65
Burr, Borden, 48–49, 51
Burton, Harold, 251
Butler, John, 126–27

Caesar, Julius, 32
Campbell, Lizzie Mae, 178, 179
Campbell, Spencer, 164–66, 178, 198–99, 251, 255
Camus, Albert, 158
Canterbury Methodist Church, 172
Cardozo, Benjamin, 119, 195
Chaplin, Charlie, 49
Christian Science, 169
Cicero, 134, 248, 253
CIO Southern Organizing Committee, 149, 150
Civil War, 32, 73
Civitan Club, 24
Clay County, 3–14, 17
Coates, Gladys, 202
Cole, Nat King, 211
Columbia Law School, 241
Common Law (Holmes), 117, 118–19
Confucius, 174
Congressional Library, 160, 235
Connor, Bull, 213
Constitutional Faith, A (Black), 123–24
"Contentment" (Plutarch), 159
Cooper, Jerome "Buddy," 149, 150–52, 207, 211, 212, 214

Corcoran Art Gallery, 171
Crawford, Kenneth, 119

Dade County Law Library, 220
Daniels, Sam, 219
Darr, Virginia "Tilla," 124–25
Darwin, Charles, 66
Dauphin Island, 87
Davies, Rev. A. Powell, 204
Davis, David J., 21, 26
DeMeritte, Elizabeth, *see* Black, Mrs. Hugo (Elizabeth DeMeritte)
DeMeritte, Fred, 255
Denson, Bill, 50–52
Depression of 1929, 155
Dialogus (Tacitus), 134
Dickens, Dr. Paul, 112, 178
Dokies (organization), 24
Dostoevsky, Fedor, 158
Douglas, William, 184, 187, 192, 231, 235, 236, 239–45
Dulles, John Foster, 231
Durr, Ann, 129
Durr, Cliff, 162
Durr, Virginia, 38, 39, 64, 162

Eagles (organization), 24
Eddy, Mary Baker, 169
Elks (organization), 24
Essays (Plutarch), 159
Evans, Hiram, 9

Fair Labor Standards Act, 88, 152
"Fallacies of an Anti-Reformer," 160

Federal Employer's Liability Act (F.E.L.A.), 226, 227, 230, 231
Field Artillery Division (World War I), 31
Fifth Circuit Judicial Conference, 197
First Amendment, 138, 176, 183–85, 186, 232, 236
First Baptist Church (Birmingham), 24
Foot, Dr., 89, 90
Fort Sill, 32
Fortas, Abe, 72
Foster, Josephine, *see* Black, Mrs. Hugo (Josephine Foster)
Foster, Dr. Sterling J., 38, 63–75, 164, 207
Foster, Mrs. Sterling J. (Anne "Nana"), 38, 64, 74, 75
Foster, Sterling, Jr., 39, 64
Foster, Virginia, *see* Durr, Virginia
Foster family, 38, 63–75
Fourteenth Amendment, 175, 236, 242, 258
Frank, Jerome, 231
Frankfurter, Felix, 137, 187, 191, 223–38, 239, 258
Frankfurter, Marion, 229
Freud, Sigmund, 158

Gaius Gracchus, 159
George, Mr. and Mrs. Walter, 80
George Washington Hospital, 261, 262

Georgia Power Company, 80
Gibbon, Edward, 158
Gibson, White, 45
Go East, Young Man (Douglas), 240
Goldberg, Arthur J., 149, 151–52, 243
Goldsmith, Oliver, 157
Government Printing Office, 266
Gracián's *Manual*, 175
Grant, Hugh, 100
Great Diablo, The (circus performer), 147
Greek Way, The (Hamilton), 159
Green, Cooper, 68–69
Grubb, William "Billy," 21, 22–23, 54–55

Hamilton, Alexander, 144
Hamilton, Edith, 159
Harlan, John, 208, 249, 250, 254, 257–62, 263
Harrison, Rex, 123
Harvard Classics, 159–60
Harvard Law Journal, 226
Harvard Law School, 223, 231, 232, 235
Heflin, Harrington P., 27, 28
Hemingway, Ernest, 158
Hill, Lister, 108, 206
Hill, Mrs. Lister, 108
Hirohito, Emperor, 67
Hitler, Adolf, 73
Hogate's (restaurant), 108
Holmes, Oliver Wendell, 117, 118–19, 195, 223, 227, 232

Horace Mann School, 95
Hughes, Charles Evans, 188
Hutchins, Robert, 241

Jackson, Robert, 190–91
Jalal ud-din Rumi, 240
Jefferson, Thomas, 96, 143, 154, 157, 158, 180
Jefferson County, Ala., 27, 28, 59, 212
Johnson, Andrew, 158
Johnson, Mr. and Mrs. Hiram, 80
Johnston, Forney, 31
Joyce, James, 158
Judicial Process (Cardozo), 119

Kafka, Franz, 158
Kaniksu National Forest, 87
Kelly, Paige & Black (law firm), 221
Kilby, Tom, 60
Kilby Steel Company, 60
Kirkegaard, Søren, 158
Kiwanis Club, 24
Knights of Pythias, 24
Korean War, 32
Ku Klux Klan, 62, 101, 103, 104, 105, 190, 215, 216

Lackey, 7–8
Lamb, Frances, 255
Lane, A. O., 21, 22–23
Lee, Robert E., 4
LeHand, Missy, 101, 102
Lewis, Jim "Ham," 80–81
Lewis, John L., 67

Life of John Marshall (Beveridge), 158
Lilburne, John, 81
Lives (Plutarch), 159
Llewellyn, Karl, 119
Logic (Mill), 119
Long, Huey "the Kingfish," 76–78
Look (magazine), 231
Lynne, Seyborne, 203

McAdoo, William Gibbs, 80–81
Macaulay, Thomas, 65
McCarran, Pat, 83
McCarran amendment, 83–84
McCarthy, Joseph, 72, 235
MacDuff, Wilbur, 220
McFarland, Ernest "Mac," 56–57
Machiavelli, Niccolò, 175
McKellar, Kenneth, 160
McReynolds, James Clark, 231, 243
Madison, James, 157
Main Currents in American Thought (Parrington), 159
Maine, Sir Henry, 53
Mann, Thomas, 158
Manush, Henry "Heinie," 96
Marble, Mary, 42
Marcus Aurelius, 113, 159, 243
Marshall, John, 182, 243, 244
Marshall, Thurgood, 243
Masons (organization), 24
Matisse, Henri, 171

Melville, Herman, 158
Mill, John Stuart, 119
Milton, John, 157
Misérables, Les (Hugo), 9
Mitch, Bill, 149, 152, 214
Mohammedanism, 174
Mullins, Clarence, 46
Murphy, Frank, 229, 242
Musgrove, Breck, 60
My Fair Lady, 123

National Industrial Recovery Act, 82–83
National Labor Relations Board (NLRB), 150, 152
New Deal, 216
New York Times, The, 213–14
Nick Carter (magazine), 9
Nixon, Richard M., 242, 244–45, 248, 265
Norris, George, 78, 81
Nuremberg trials, 190

Oberdorfer, Lou, 248, 252
"On Old Age" (Cicero), 248, 253
Orator (Cicero), 134
Oyster School (Washington, D.C.), 89, 97

Parrington, Vernon Louis, 140, 159
Patrick, Luther, 207, 208
Patterson, Ann, *see* Foster, Mrs. Sterling J.
Patterson, Col. Josiah, 38
Patterson, Lizzie, 9
Patterson, Malcolm, 38

Pearl Harbor Commission, 189, 190
Peloponnesian War (Thucydides), 158
Pentagon Papers, 138, 246
Plessy v. Ferguson, 208
Plutarch, 159
Poetics (Aristotle), 134, 137
Pollution Department (Alexandria, Va.), 255
Primitive Baptist Church, 3, 10
Prince, The (Machiavelli), 175
Prohibition, 62
Proust, Marcel, 158
Public Works Administration, 83

Quest for Law (Crawford), 119

Randolph, General H. Lee, 33–36, 56, 190
Ray, Ben, 28–30
Redmen (organization), 24
Reed, Stanley, 132, 134
Remembrance Rock (Sandburg), 157
Rhetoric (Aristotle), 134, 137
Rise and Fall of the Roman Empire, The (Gibbon), 158
Roberts, Owen J., 189–90, 195
Robinson, Joe, 76, 77
Rodell, Fred, 119
Roman Catholic Church, 104, 176
Roosevelt, Franklin D., 82, 83–84, 100, 101–3, 114, 145, 189, 216, 223

Rousseau, Jean-Jacques, 53
Rutledge, Wiley, 228–29, 242

Sacco and Vanzetti trial, 224
Sandburg, Carl, 157
School of Arts and Sciences (University of Alabama), 16
Seay, Mrs., 246, 247
Securities and Exchange Commission, 241
Senate Ladies Luncheon Club, 80
Shakespeare, William, 157
Sherman Anti-Trust Act, 82
Shintoism, 174
Shuttlesworth, Fred, 213
Smith, C. B., 36, 48–50, 51–52
Social Contract (Rousseau), 53
Socrates, 128
Sophocles, 157
South Highlands Presbyterian Church, 64
Sparkman, John, 206
Steed, Charley, 8
Stone, Harlan Fiske, 190
Study of History (Toynbee), 158
Sturges, Wesley A., 133, 241
Swarthmore College, 124, 158, 179
Sweet Briar Academy, 38
Sweet Briar College, 38, 124

Tacitus, 134
Taoism, 174
Tate, Joe, 31
Taylor, J. K. "Jake," 47
Tennessee Coal, Iron, and Railroad Company, 44, 45

Textile Workers Union of America, 150–51
Thoreau, Henry David, 154
Thucydides, 158
Tiberius, 159
Toland, John Breckenridge "Uncle Brack," 12–13
Topics (Aristotle), 120, 134
Tort Claims Division (Department of Justice), 219
Tortoricci, Mary, 202
Toynbee, Arnold, 158
Truman, Harry, 190, 191

Unitarian Church, 204
United Mine Workers, 67
U.S. Constitution, 101, 175, 182, 183, 236, 266
U.S. Court of Appeals, 71
U.S. Department of Justice, 145, 218–19
U.S. District Court, 46
U.S. Forest Service, 87
U.S. Senate, 58–62, 76–88, 91, 99–100, 153, 162, 206
U.S. Steel Corporation, 44
U.S. Supreme Court, 66, 83, 99–105, 106, 114, 135, 145, 149, 152, 153, 159, 162, 169, 182–92, 199, 200, 201, 208–9, 215, 223–25, 226–50, 258, 260
United Steelworkers of America, 149, 152, 211
University of Alabama, 16, 115, 206, 215

University of Alabama Law School, 16, 17

Van Devanter, Willis, 182
Veterans of Foreign Wars, 32
Vietnam war, 32
Vinson, Fred, 190, 229
Virginia Episcopal Seminary, 162

Waggaman, 179
Warren, Earl, 229, 242, 243, 245, 252
Washington *News*, 96
Washington *Post*, 264
Washington Senators, 96
Washington *Star*, 264
Webster's Dictionary, 117, 135
Whatley, Barney, 17, 19–21
White, Gertrude, 91
Woe Unto You Lawyers (Rodell), 119
Woodmen of the World (organization), 24
World War I, 31, 38, 81
World War II, 66, 144

Yale Law Journal, 132, 133
Yale Law School, 121, 132–34, 206, 230, 235, 241
Yale Law School Student Association, 133
Yale University, 132–33
Yancey, William, 73
Yancy, George, 47–48

Zog, King, 100